# A SPIRIT OF ENQUIRY
## *Essays for Ted Wright*

edited by

**John Coles**
**Valerie Fenwick**
**Gillian Hutchinson**

*published by*

| | | |
|---|---|---|
| *Wetland Archaeology Research Project* | ✧ *Nautical Archaeology Society* | ✧ *National Maritime Museum* |

*with the support of*

| | |
|---|---|
| *Fenland Archaeological Trust* | ✧ *Somerset Levels Project* |

*1993*

First published in 1993 by
Wetland Archaeology Research Project,
Nautical Archaeology Society and
National Maritime Museum

ISBN 0-9519117-1-6

WARP Occasional Paper 7
ISSN 1350-2832

*Cover photograph: Ted Wright on the foreshore
at Ferriby.*

*Photo: John Coles*

Typeset by WARP, Department of History and
Archaeology, University of Exeter.

Printed in the U.K. by Short Run Press Ltd., Exeter.

# CONTENTS

# PREFACE

Ted Wright's contribution to boat and wetland archaeology has been crucial to the development of new ideas and new projects over many years. Equally important is his enthusiasm for the subjects, infectious and always encouraging. Those who have been taken on a tour of the foreshore on the Humber at Ferriby are unlikely to forget that enthusiasm, nor their lost gumboots.

When the Dover boat was first displayed to an eager audience of archaeologists in December 1992, with Ted much in evidence in the discussions that followed, the idea of some sort of offering of essays came to mind. Support for the idea was soon promised by the Wetland Archaeology Research Project, the Nautical Archaeology Society and the National Maritime Museum, all of which have had the benefit of Ted's association over many years. Our first approaches to potential contributors brought such a response that additional financial support had to be requested from the Fenland Archaeological Trust and the Somerset Levels Project, and instantly granted.

We are grateful for all of this support, and offer these essays to Ted in appreciation for his contributions to our studies.

*Acknowledgement.*
The editors extend their thanks to Mike Rouillard of the Department of History and Archaeology, University of Exeter, for undertaking all of the DTP work for this book.

J.M.C.
V.F.
G.H.

# 1

# LOGBOATS OF THE 6TH MILLENNIUM BC DISCOVERED IN SWITZERLAND

## *Béat Arnold*

In earlier work we analysed Swiss logboats dating from the Late Bronze Age (10 items, Arnold 1985), from the Late La Tène and the Roman period (Arnold 1992), as well as from modern times (Arnold 1983).

Here we examine the oldest logboats discovered in Switzerland. They date from the transitional period between the Early and Middle Neolithic. Two were found in Lake Neuchâtel, at Auvernier and Hauterive, and a third one in Lake Zurich at Männedorf. All three are carved out of lime (*Tilia*), a soft homogeneous species which was also used a great deal in Denmark between 6000 and 4500 BP, during the last phases of the Mesolithic (Ertebølle culture) and the beginning of the Neolithic in that region (Rieck and Crumlin-Pederson 1988). This was not the only species used at that time however; the logboats recently discovered in Paris-Bercy are all made out of oak (*Quercus*).

These boats are contemporaneous with the forests of the Atlantic period, characterized by the expansion of mixed oak groves where oak (*Quercus*), elm (*Ulmus*) and lime (*Tilia*) dominate. Towards the end of this phase, fir (*Abies*), alder (*Alnus*) and beech (*Fagus*) appear and they continue to develop during the following phase, the Sub-Boreal, which includes the Recent Neolithic and the Bronze Age. Pine (*Pinus*), which had dominated the forests of the Allerød and the Pre-Boreal almost exclusively, gave way to the hazel (*Corylus*) and mixed oak groves at the beginning of the Boreal. During the Atlantic, it was the mixed oak forest alone which dominated. Pine did not disappear, rather it attained an equilibrium similar to that of today.

We should mention that for the period before 6000 BP, we only know of the mesolithic logboat from Noyen-sur-Seine (Seine-et-Marne; 7960 ± 100 BP, Gif-6559; Mordant 1987), to which we could add the wooden object of Pesse (Drenthe; 8265 ± 275 BP, Gro-486; Zeist1957), although it may not necessarily be part of a logboat

considering its slight dimensions. Both artefacts, made of pine (*Pinus*), can be more or less situated in the transitional period between the Boreal and the Early Atlantic.

We are using the BP data for the values obtained by C-14 analysis; the BC dates are used exclusively for the dendrochronological results (based on the references of Becker *et al.* 1985).

## *Hauterive-Champréveyres 1976*

The Hauterive logboat was first sighted by a diver in 1976 in the western part of what was to become a vast polder in 1983 when the area was completely drained in order to carry out an emergency excavation at Champréveyres. This excavation revealed a Magdalenian campsite, a Middle Neolithic village ("Cortaillod classique", 3810-3790 BC), part of a Late Neolithic site and a large Late Bronze Age settlement which was inhabited for almost two centuries (*Archéologie neuchâteloise*, vol.7 and following). Two dates are given for this logboat: 5280 ± 50 BP (B-4771) and 5540 ± 60 BP (B-4529).

When the two dates are put together, they cover a time lapse of approximately one or two centuries between the wood sample taken from this boat and the establishment of the first littoral villages of the region (3867 BC for Montilier-Dorf, on Lake Morat). This interval should be reduced again by half, considering the many tree rings removed while carving the boat.

Even though this boat was found only 6 metres from the palisade encircling the "Cortaillod classique" village, the stratigraphical context is not precise enough and far too eroded to provide any information (Rychner-Faraggi 1987).

The incomplete logboat was substantially reduced by lake erosion between 1976 and 1983: its length dwindled from 5,16m to 4,85m for a width of 0,52m (Pl.1.1, fig.1.1).

Marks made by the tools used to carve the dugout are very worn and can only be seen under oblique light on the

bear axe marks which were partially grown over before the tree was cut down and converted into posts. We have no clear answer as to what this preliminary work involved nor what exactly the prehistoric inhabitants tried to achieve by it. Concerning the lime used for the logboat, no axe marks

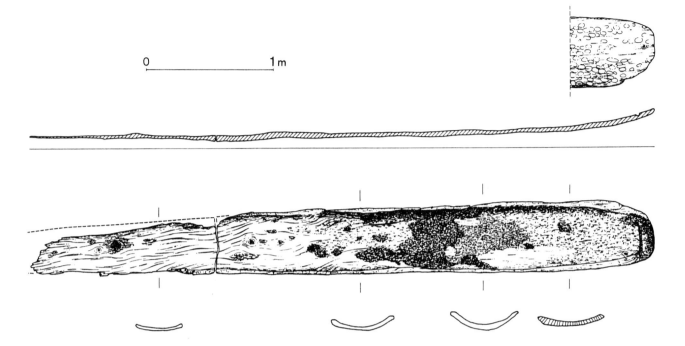

*Fig. 1.1   Drawing, in situ, of the Hauterive-1976 logboat. Rémy Wenger*

underside of the preserved end. On the upper side, a transversal groove 3cm wide, narrowing to 1,5cm at the bottom, was carved in the floor of the boat to receive a small separate plank closing off the boat at the back. There are no tool marks visible on the inside of the logboat: they were all effaced either intentionally or with use. The bottom was also partially burnt at a later date but not as a method of hollowing it out, contrary to that observed in certain logboats from Paris-Bercy where zones were heavily charred then hewn with an axe or an adze.

The preserved end, which by comparison to other Late Bronze Age discoveries made in the same lake and in Denmark (eg. Øgårde 3) can be identified as the stern, has tool marks on its underside very similar to those found on the posts in the Neolithic villages. These marks are made by polished stone axes or adzes cut and prepared from ophite blocks.

When the boat was turned over, after a cast had been made of its upper side, it was discovered that the knots observed on the inside were not present on the outside: the branches had been removed and the last tree rings had completely grown over the scars. Is this an indication that the tree, selected to become a dugout later on, underwent preliminary work while still standing, or were the branches simply stripped off this side of the lime by the fall of a neighbouring tree?

Several posts at the nearby "Cortaillod classique" site

could be clearly identified where the branches had been stripped. Since almost 50 annual rings covered the scars [note1], it would seem that the stripped branches were the result of a natural accident. If this were not the case, one would have to imagine a well established group engaging in a kind of silvaculture along the shore for more than half a century in spite of the absence of villages here; unless, of course, the branches were removed for another use such as fodder for example.

Future discoveries will hopefully help to establish whether man really did engage in very long-term management of trees intended for logboats.

## *Auvernier 1973*

Another logboat was discovered in the archaeological layers of the site at Auvernier-Port in 1973. It lay at the surface of the layers belonging to a "Cortaillod classique" habitat, beneath a layer of lake sediments covered by a "Cortaillod tardif" site (Billamboz *et al.* 1982, 35, fig.12). If we transform the dendrochronological dates given for this site (Becker *et al.* 1985, 50) into uncalibrated C-14 dates, we obtain 5200-5000 BP for this habitat and thus for the boat.

Only a small part of the bottom, 2,17m long and 0,52m wide, remained (fig.1.2). The outer surface is flat and the sides are more or less cylindrical. The tool marks are particularly clear. Arranged in parallel strips as long as

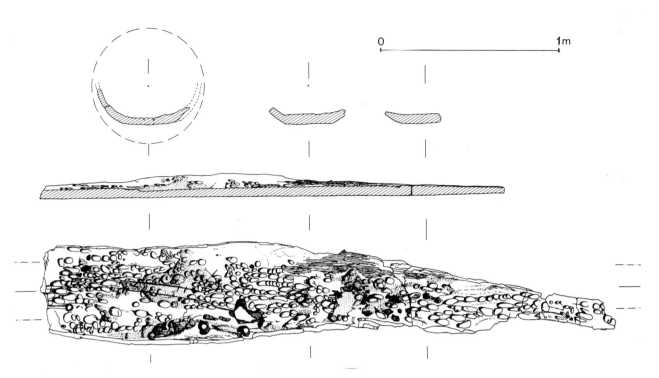

*Fig. 1.2 Drawing of the Auvernier-1973 logboat.*

30-50cm, they are shaped like elongated cups having a maximum width of 3cm and a length of 4-6cm (pl.1.2). Certain gouges are partially or totally obliterated by fire but this happened after the boat had been made (Arnold 1980, 179-180).

## Männedorf 1977

The first logboat mentioned here was studied *in situ* and a cast was made of it before it was turned over in segments to reveal the underside. The bottom of the second logboat was observed after it was removed from the lake sediments, whereas the third one was taken out of the lake with the surrounding sediments in large lifting frames and transported to the laboratory. In spite of our request, we were not given the opportunity to analyse it at that time and no drawings were made of it. As the process of conservation turned out to be problematic, the entire analysis is based on two small fragments which were saved, a few photographs made in the laboratory after it was cleaned (pl.1.3) and a sketch of its contours executed by the divers who discovered it (Hasenfratz and Ruoff 1979). Although this logboat appears to be one of the most complete, comprising very fresh tool marks, the preserved elements unfortunately only allow us to propose a rough outline of it.

Its length when discovered was 5,95m and its maximum width 0,5m. Based upon the laboratory photographs and the two preserved fragments, the boat was originally about 7,30m long, 0,60m wide and 0,24m high (fig.1.3). Its section is slightly oval and its outer surface resembles a polygon following the natural curve of the trunk, at least on the two surviving pieces. This logboat was also carved out of lime. It is dated to 5490± 50 BP (UCLA-2706B; Arnold *et al.* 1988).

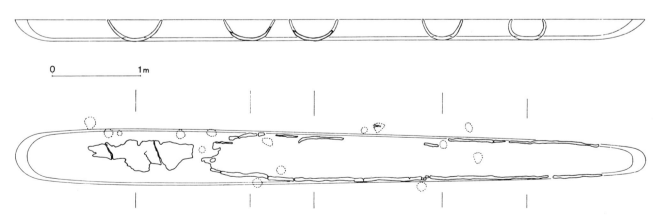

*Fig. 1.3 Reconstruction of the Männedorf-1977 logboat, with a heavier line outlining the parts mapped by the divers.*

## Conclusions

These three logboats, together with those of Denmark, prove indubitably that lime was the preferred choice of wood out of which to make logboats between 6300 and 5000 BP, although the oak logboats discovered at Paris-Bercy show that this choice was not exclusive. Later on, oak became the preferred species. The possibility that some kind of management of trees intended for logboats was already being carried out at that time should not be excluded. As we have seen, the charred areas on the bottom of these canoes are not necessarily the result of hollowing out the trunk with fire but can be due to secondary burning as in the case of the Auvernier-1973 and the Hauterive-1976 dugouts. This can be established by careful observation of the relationship between the tool marks and the charred areas.

## Note

1] Hauterive-1976: Werner Schoch's report of 11.12.1985 ("Swiss federal Institute of forestry research"), indicates that the number of growth rings after these branches were stripped varies between 47 and 60.

*Acknowledgements.* I would like to thank Daniel Pillonel for his helpful remarks and Janet Lechmann McCallion for this translation.

## References

Arnold, B. 1980. Navigation sur le lac de Neuchâtel: une esquisse à travers le temps. *Helvetia Archaeologica* 11, n°. 43/44, 178-195.

Arnold, B. 1983. Les dernières pirogues monoxyles de Suisse centrale. *Helvetia Archaeologica* 14, n°. 55/56, 271-286.

Arnold, B. 1985. Navigation et construction navale sur les lacs suisses au Bronze final. *Helvetia Archaeologica* 16, n°. 63/64, 91-117

Arnold, B. 1992. *Batellerie gallo-romaine sur le lac de Neuchâtel*, vol. 1 and 2. Archéologica neuchâteloise 12 et 13. Saint-Blaise: Editions du Ruau.

Arnold, B. *et al.* 1988. Radiocarbon dating of six Swiss watercraft. *Int. J. Naut. Archaeol.* 17/2, 183-186.

Becker, B. *et al* 1985. *Dendrochronologie in der Ur- und Frühgeschichte. Die absolute Datierung von Pfahlbausiedlungen nördlich der Alpen im Jahrringkalender Mitteleuropas.* Antiqua 11. Basel: Schweizerische Gesellschraft für Ur- und Frühgeschichte.

Billamboz, A. *et al.* 1982. *La station littorale d'Auvernier-Port. Cadre et évolution.* Cahiers d'archéologie romande 25, Auvernier 5. Laussane: Bibliothèque historique vaudoise.

Hasenfratz, A. and Ruoff, U. 1979. Ein verziertes neolithisches Gefäss aus Männedorf ZH. *Annuaire de la Société suisse de préhistoire et d'archéologie* 63, 7-12.

Mordant, C. and D. 1987. Noyen-sur Seine, site mésolithique en milieu humide fluviatile. In: *112e Congrès national des Sociétés savantes (Lyon, 1987)*, Pré- protohistoire, 33-52. Paris: Bibliothèque nationale.

Rieck, F. and Crumlin-Pederson, O. 1988. *Både fra Danmarks oldtid.* Roskilde: Vikingeskibshallen.

Rychner-Farraggi, A.-M. 1987. Un village néolithique à Hauterive-Champréveyres. In: Hauterive a 12000 ans. *Nouvelle revue neuchâteloise* 4, n°.15, 23-36.

Zeist, W. van 1957. De mesolithische boot van Pesse. *Nieuwe Drentse Volksalmanak* 75, 4-11.

# 2

# INTERTIDAL ARCHAEOLOGY AT GOLDCLIFF IN THE SEVERN ESTUARY

## Martin Bell

Only recently has the Severn Estuary emerged as an area of major intertidal archaeological potential, comparable perhaps to the potential long established in the Humber Estuary by Ted Wright (1990a). Many of these new discoveries, including the Goldcliff site discussed here, have been made by an individual fieldworker, Mr Derek Upton of Caldicot. On the foreshore at Uskmouth and Magor Pill, tracks of human footprints have been found in clays sealed by peats which date the footprints to the later Mesolithic (Aldhouse-Green *et al.* forthcoming). A water-logged later Bronze Age roundhouse has been recorded on intertidal peat at Chapeltump and another waterlogged Bronze Age site at Cold Harbour (Whittle 1989). In addition there is the waterlogged riverine Bronze Age site at Caldicot (Nayling 1992). The Roman and later archae-ology of the Severn Estuary has similarly been transformed by the work of Allen and Fulford (1986) who have demon-strated that large areas of the former estuary claylands were reclaimed during the Romano-British period. Recent research on the line of the Second Severn Crossing has produced evidence of late Saxon and Medieval wooden fish traps which are closely comparable to those in use in the estuary until recently (Godbold and Turner 1992). The Severn Estuary Levels Research Committee (1990-92) plays a liaison and coordinating role and has published three annual reports summarising archaeological research in the estuary, much of it prompted by natural erosion and an increasing number of development threats. The Goldcliff project is part of this broader endeavour; it aims to inves-tigate the archaeological and palaeoenvironmental se-quence of the intertidal zone. The area surveyed so far is 1.5 km of coast (fig.2.1), representing 0.8 % of the whole estuary coast. This area surveyed in detail has proved to be remarkably rich in archaeology of several periods.

## Mesolithic site

Adjacent to the bedrock rise of Goldcliff which, at times of maximum marine influence would have been an island some 350 by 200m, is evidence of Mesolithic activity (fig.2.1). This consists of a charcoal-rich Holocene surface buried by estuarine clay, then fen peat. A radiocarbon date for the charcoal is 6430 ± 80 BP (GU-2759). The charcoal layer contains worked flint and chert, also bones of red deer, pig, wolf, fox and cat (B. Noddle, *pers. comm.*). Thin charcoal bands separated by marine clays have also been found in a trench excavated to investigate the interface between the bedrock island and wetland behind the present seawall at Hill Farm. Here the charcoal layer contained flints, one a microlith, and bones. It remains to be estab-lished from pollen and other palaeoenvironmental re-search whether this Mesolithic charcoal derives from domestic hearths or larger-scale woodland burning. A pollen diagram from 600m east of Goldcliff (Smith and Morgan 1989) shows evidence of three episodes of anthropogenic impact following the elm decline. This evidence for significant human impact on either side of 5000 uncalibrated BC means that the site has particular potential for investigation of the Mesolithic / Neolithic transition.

## Bronze Age Boat Planks

Some 330m west of the intertidal Mesolithic site a small platform-like structure was located. This measured 1.6 by 1.3m and comprised two planks, some cut roundwood and pieces of brushwood held in place by several pegs (pl. 2.1). The structure was in a clay layer but above and below it were thin reed peats. It could have been made to cross a wet patch or to provide a dry area for some particular activity

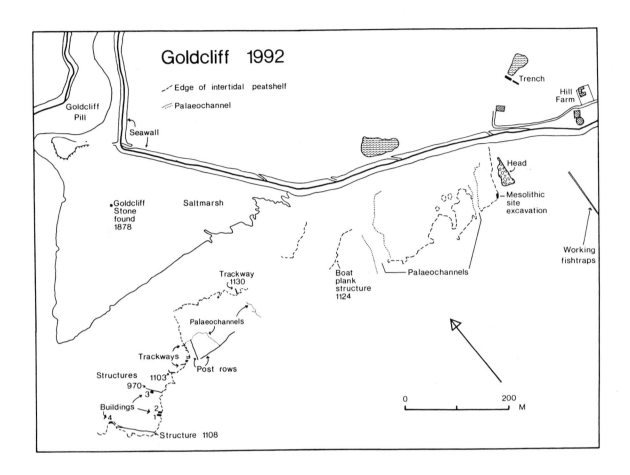

*Fig. 2.1 Goldcliff, Wales. The intertidal area, showing the location of peat shelves and wooden structures, and the Mesolithic site.*

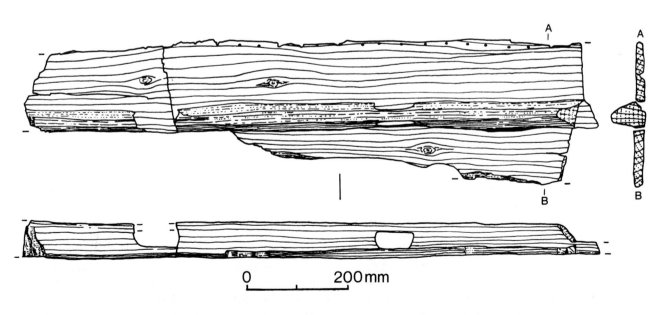

*Fig. 2.2 Goldcliff, Wales. Boat plank 3436 from Bronze Age structure 1124.*

such as hunting, fishing or fowling. A piece of roundwood from this structure has a radiocarbon date of 2720±70 BP(CAR-1434). The two planks make this structure of particular interest. Each had a raised ridge down the axis through which, in the case of plank 3436 (fig. 2.2), two sub-rectangular mortises had been cut. Down the margins of the planks were closely spaced holes, *c.*4-6mm in diameter, most of them still containing plant fibre cord. There is little doubt that these are planks from a middle Bronze Age sewn boat, the same family of craft as the Ferriby boats discovered by Ted Wright (1990b), the recently discovered Dover boat (Parfitt 1993) and the boat plank from Caldicot, nearby in the Severn Estuary (Parry and McGrail 1991). Once its original life was over, boat plank 3438 (not illustrated) had a mortise hole of diameter 4cm cut; and its later use as part of the platform structure did not make use of the mortise hole, which presumably therefore relates to a preceding secondary use of the timber.

## Rectangular buildings

The main concentration of prehistoric archaeology at Goldcliff relates to a single prominent peat shelf that is exposed to varying extents below the shifting mud of the estuary. To seaward the shelf is truncated by erosion and to landward it is buried by estuarine clays. The width of the shelf is about 5m, rather wider where there are rectangular structures and linear post alignments which tend to be associated with slight rises in the peat.

Rectangular timber Buildings 1 and 2 (fig. 2.3) have been excavated totally. Both were partly truncated on the south east side by erosion associated with the peat edge, here only the longer, more substantial timbers survived. Building 1 was 8.4 by 5.6m with rounded corners and slightly bowed end walls and a single surviving 60 cm wide entrance on the north side. The walls were of roundwood, about 10 cm in diameter and pointed with an iron axe. Between these were roundwood wattles about 3cm in diameter which had been cut and pointed by a single diagonal axe blow. The latter were at about 45 degrees to the verticals and are interpreted as wattles which had been woven round the vertical elements. Down the central axis of the building were two substantial roundwood verticals each with a surrounding packing of smaller posts and wedges. The presence of these here, and in the other rectangular structures (noted below), leaves little doubt that they are the remains of roofed buildings. Flooring was preserved in the north west corner, it was unmodified roundwood, laid diagonally to the corner (pl. 2.2). In this, the most well-preserved part of the building, there were two internal partitions delimiting areas 70cm wide and reminiscent of animal stalls. The building was also divided into two equal halves by a post partition. Its entrance was consolidated by woodchips from the working of oak timbers. Radiocarbon dates for Building 1 are 2100±60 BP (CAR-1346) and 2120±90 BP (GU-2912). Building 2 was parallel and separated by a 50 cm alley. It was 5.2 by 7.4 m, a little smaller than its neighbour, with a 90 cm wide entrance slightly set back.

The walls were of vertical posts with little evidence of wattles. Four large posts with packing were present down the long axis, one pair probably replacing the others. Flooring of rather rough unmodified roundwood survived in the north corner and there was no evidence of internal subdivisions. Radiocarbon dates for Building 2 are 2160±70 BP (CAR-1348) and 2220 ±60 BP (CAR-1352).

Five other buildings of the same general type have also been planned. Building 3 is 35m north of Building 1; three of its walls are buried by the overlying grey clay and its dimensions are uncertain. One wall post has been radiocarbon dated 2200± 70 BP (CAR-1437). The roundwood floor is intact. Structure 4 had been partly cut away by erosion; it measured 7.2m long with rounded corners and bowed end walls. No axial roof supports remained and little flooring. The walls comprised roundwood verticals one of which has been radiocarbon dated 2140±60BP (CAR-1435).

On what may be a continuation of the same peat shelf to the west, Structure 6 was found. It wall lines were complete; it was rectangular with rounded corners 7m by 5m and probable entrances in the middle of the shorter walls. There were two axial post settings which are interpreted as roof supports. The method of construction was roundwood verticals about every 60cm between which the wall was formed of radially split timbers, some of which were planks. No flooring survived but there were some internal posts. The building was on a slightly raised area of peat, the edges of which were defined in places by a palaeochannel with clay fill. This contained a twisted withy tie, a lath of worked wood and some bones. 44 m away Structure 7 comprised just 13 posts forming a rough rectangle 4.8 by 4.2 m, down the axis of which were two larger posts suggesting that this too may be the truncated remains of a roofed building of the same general type. Structure 8 was 190m west of Structure 7; it was rectangular with rounded corners 6 by 8m. Once again there was evidence of two post settings down the long axis. The walls were formed of rather irregularly spaced vertical split timbers and roundwood without any surviving flooring. The structure was on a slightly raised area of peat, the edges of which were defined by shallow palaeochannel features forming part of a net-like pattern. The channel fill was peat and on the surface of this were many hundreds of animal footprints.

## Linear wood structures

On the same peat shelf as Buildings 1-4 were a number of linear wooden structures (fig. 2.1), the longest (1108) running from Structure 4 100m south. It comprised two rough alignments of small posts 20-30cm apart. On excavation these proved to have been driven in diagonally from alternate sides. In the V-shaped area created by these diagonal posts was brushwood, some roundwood and planking. Provisionally this is interpreted as a trackway running from Structure 4 towards the estuary. One of the posts is dated 2140±60 BP (CAR-1436), the same date as that for Structure 4. Another row of posts (970) ran beside

11

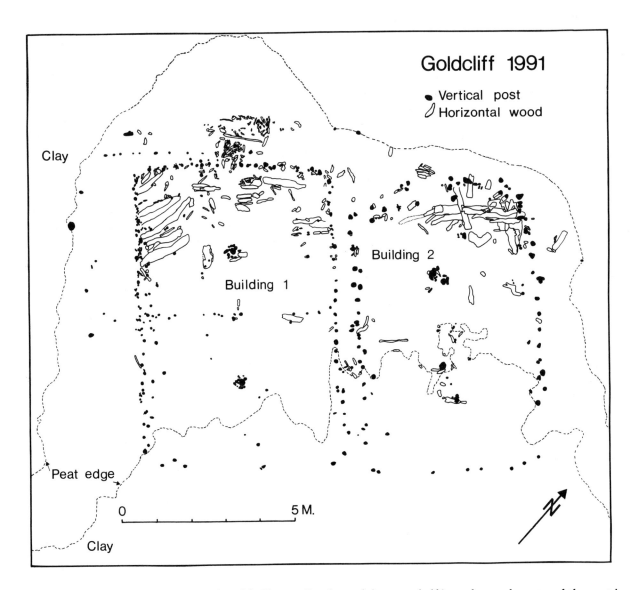

*Fig. 2.3 Goldcliff, Wales. Buildings 1 and 2. The eroding face of the peat shelf is to the south-east and the peat is overlain by clay to the west and north.*

Building 3. Here the timbers were vertical, about 40cm apart. That seems too narrow for a track, and flooring material was absent, its function remains enigmatic. A post is radiocarbon dated 2190±60 BP (CAR-1439). Structure 1103 was more complex and comprised several alignments of small vertical posts with brushwood along the axis of the structure, in places apparently woven round the verticals. The most likely interpretation seems to be as superimposed phases of some form of trackway or fence. Nearby seven trackways of a different type were revealed along just 44m of the eroding peat face. The clearest of these comprise brushwood about 50cm wide held in place by roundwood laterals pegged on the outside. Others comprise only brushwood or contain more roundwood along the axis of the track. Trackways 1 and 8 have been traced below the overlying clay where they are much better preserved. Radiocarbon dates for Trackway 1: 2260±60BP (CAR-1349) and Trackway 3: 2290±60 BP(CAR- 1350) show that they are broadly contemporary with the rectangular buildings to their west. Trackway 1130 was 145m

east of the group of seven and of contrasting type. It was 0.9m wide of roundwood laid corduroy fashion at right angles to the line of the track and held in place by pegs.

## Conclusions

Seven rectangular buildings have been found at Goldcliff, the four with radiocarbon dates are closely similar; in calibrated terms, using the curve of Stuiver and Pearson (1986) they are in the last four centuries BC. The trackways and double post row (970) for which dates are available are of similar date. The rectangular buildings are virtually unique in the British Iron Age when the vast majority of structures are round houses. The general form of the Goldcliff buildings is closer to those recorded from the continental Iron Age (eg Audouze and Buchsenschutz 1992).

As regards the environmental setting of the structures, laboratory work is only in its early stages; provisional points can, however, be made on the basis of field observations. The peat around the rectangular buildings had treestumps of alder and birch. Some of the fen woodland in which they were situated was cut down for the making of the structures, cut timbers lay in the peat and the predominant tree types used in Buildings 1 and 2 were alder and birch, although other types were also brought from further away (S. Johnson *pers. comm.*), some of them apparently for repairs. There is evidence that during the period over which the buildings were subject to repair the site was episodically inundated by the sea, thin layers of blue clay being found within the occupation horizon. The beetle evidence complements this picture with much evidence of species associated with detrital decaying plant material at the margins of water (P. Osborne *pers. comm.*). The main concentration of brushwood trackways, east of the buildings, was not in woodland but a wetter area of reed swamp.

It seems unlikely that the buildings were permanently occupied domestic structures, as none contained hearths or charcoal. The only non-wood artifacts from the excavated Buildings 1 and 2 were a single bone within Building 1 and a scatter of bones outside, mostly around the entrances. Those identified so far are cattle, some neonatal, sheep, horse and deer (B. Noddle *pers. comm.*). The evidence for episodic marine inundation supports the idea of seasonal activity. One possibility is grazing of animals, as suggested by the many footprints around Structure 8 and the hint of stalls within Structure 1. Work on the beetles from Building 1 (P. Osborne *pers. comm.*) has not, however, so far produced evidence of dung. Another possibility is that the structures related to fishing activities. There is today a salmon fishery at Goldcliff which has been documented since the fourteenth century, but so far no fish bones have been found in the sieving. Equally it is possible that this concentration of activity was associated with fowling, a crossing place of the Severn or with ritual or symbolic activities. The merit of this site, and indeed of other wetland intertidal sites, is that the stratigraphic resolution, organic preservation and range of palaeoenvironmental evidence is so good as to provide a realistic chance of evaluating the relative strengths of these various working hypotheses.

When trying to picture what life would have been like in this wet, episodically inundated landscape it is profitable to read W. Thesinger's (1985) account of life among the Marsh Arabs of southern Iraq in 1951-58. He described and photographed substantial rectangular buildings, in this case of reeds, set on slight rises surrounded by water. It was a way of life based on the water, the keeping of cattle, hunting, fowling and fishing. The analogue is in no sense precise but at least it helps to broaden our own limited experience of such different ways of life. In a similar way the archaeological record also broadens our understanding of adaptation to highly specialised environments and the diversity of human existence. This is the compensation for the not insignificant logistical difficulties of working on a site covered by several metres of muddy sea twice a day.

*Acknowledgements.* The Goldcliff project is funded by Cadw, St. David's University College, The National Museum of Wales, Newport Museum and the European Social Fund. We are grateful to Mr Martin Hazell and Mr Walters for access and help. Derek Upton's contribution has been considerable and the role of Jonathan Parkhouse in first demonstrating the potential of the site is particularly acknowledged. This interim statement draws on the specialist contributions of Mr S. Allen; Mr R. Brunning; Dr J. Crowther; Dr Q. Dresser; Mrs S. Johnson; Professor S. McGrail; Ms B. Noddle and Mr P. Osborne. The student team from Lampeter and Dublin and the excavation staff are thanked for their work under difficult conditions.

## References

Aldhouse-Green, S.H.R., Whittle, A.W.R., Allen, J.R.L., Caseldine, A.E., Culver, S.J., Day, M.H., Lundquist, J. and Upton, D. Forthcoming. Prehistoric human footprints from the Severn Estuary Levels at Uskmouth and Magor Pill, Gwent, Wales.

Allen, J.R.L. and Fulford, M.G. 1986. The Wentlooge Level: a Romano-British saltmarsh reclamation in southeast Wales. *Britannia* 18, 91-117.

Andouze, F. and Buchsenschutz, O. 1992. *Towns, Villages and Countryside of Celtic Europe.* London: Batsford.

Godbold, S. and Turner, R. 1992. Second Severn Crossing 1991: Welsh Intertidal Zone. In *Severn Estuary Levels Research Committee Annual Report 1992*, Lampeter: S.E.L.R.C. 45-55.

Nayling, N. 1992. Caldicot Castle Lake. In *Severn Estuary Levels Research Committee Annual Report 1992*. Lampeter: S.E.L.R.C.11-14.

Parfitt, K. 1993. The Dover Boat. *Current Archaeology* 1993, 133, 4-8.

Parry, S.J. and McGrail, S. 1991. A prehistoric plank boat from Caldicot Castle Lake, Gwent, Wales. *Int. J. Naut. Archaeol.* 20:4, 321-324.

Severn Estuary Levels Research Committee 1990. *Annual report 1990.* Lampeter: S.E.L.R.C.

Severn Estuary Levels Research Committee 1991. *Annual report. 1991.* Lampeter: S.E.L.R.C.

Severn Estuary Levels Research Committee 1992. *Annual report 1992.* Lampeter: S.E.L.R.C.

Smith, A.G. and Morgan, L.A. 1989. A succession to ombrotrophic bog in the Gwent Levels, and its demise: a Welsh parallel to the peats of the Somerset Levels. *New Phytologist* 112, 145-167.

Stuiver, M. and Pearson, G.W. 1986. High-precision calibration of the radiocarbon timescale, AD 1950-500 BC. *Radiocarbon* 28:2B, 805-838.

Thesinger, W. 1985. *The Marsh Arabs.* London: Collins.

Whittle, A.W.R. 1989. Two later Bronze Age occupations and an Iron Age channel on the Gwent foreshore. *Bulletin of the Board of Celtic Studies* 36, 200-223.

Wright, E. 1990a. An East Yorkshire retrospective. In S. Ellis, and D.R. Crowther (eds.) 1990. *Humber Perspectives: a region through the Ages.* Hull: University Press, 71-88.

Wright, E. V. 1990b. *The Ferriby Boats. Seacraft of the Bronze Age.* London: Routledge.

# 3

# NAVAL ARCHITECTURE CAN SOMETIMES FILL THE GAPS

## *John Coates*

Archaeologists are today invoking techniques springing from the worlds of physics, chemistry, engineering, medicine, biology and indeed science generally. In investigating wrecks of ships, submerged structures and associated artefacts, nautical archaeologists are likewise turning to such disciplines not only in excavation, conservation and dating, but also in analysis and the interpretation of finds, not the least of which are the ships themselves.

Almost without exception interpretation of ship remains calls for some and often a lot of reconstruction on paper, based on what hull structure remains. Very rarely are shipwrecks found entire. Remains are in most cases confined to the lower parts of the hull, and that often deformed. Upper parts have nearly always rotted away, leaving at best a few tatters which are often in small pieces scattered about the seabed. It is common for only a part of the bottom amidships to remain. Some wrecks have fallen on to one side in coming to rest, when the other side and often more is missing: in others only one end or just the lower part of one end might have survived.

In attempting to deduce from her remains as much as possible about the complete vessel, the first aim may be to arrive at her date, dimensions and appearance in life, but of deeper interest would be her value and lifetime economics as an instrument of trade or sea power in her own time and region, her performance and capacity, seaworthiness and manner of operation, the techniques and materials of her construction, not forgetting the extent and kinds of repairs to her hull. These latter can provide informative clues about the hazards of her life or indicate the relative robustness of various parts of her structure and equipment.

Many aspects of vessels from the past are the same as, or have at least some correspondence with, the technicalities of ships today. These are in the field of naval architecture,

notwithstanding the unfamiliarity of most of its practitioners today with materials, tools and techniques, now possibly long obsolete. The essentials of many aspects of a ship or boat lie in the unchanging physical laws and so do the numerical methods based upon them by which a ship can be designed with predictable characteristics and performance. Before the acquisition of that knowledge ships could not be "designed", in our sense of the word: they could then only be developed by trial and error, and then not without risk of disaster if straying beyond any accepted and working rules of proportion.

The great changes in the materials and techniques of ship and boat building have, over the last few centuries, brought about such increases in scale and performance in ships as to make ancient vessels seem, on superficial comparison, primitive, clumsy and crude. The idea that many types of ships could, on the contrary, have been as carefully conceived and wrought for their purposes in the past as today may be buried by an assumption in many minds of some correspondence between past states of physical and technical knowledge on one hand and human intelligence and conceptual ability on the other. The knowledge may have advanced out of all recognition but it is generally agreed that the latter two attributes have been on much the same level for many millennia. That may be fairly obvious but it must follow that to think that ancient ships were as a rule primitive and crude is mistaken. Further, while established and proven designs of ships would have emerged from the process of trial-and-error to suit the needs and within the technical limits of the time, designs would also have had to respond, as they occurred, to changes of need, advances in techniques and the availability of materials, not to mention fluctuations in public and private wealth.

The phrase "shipbuilding tradition" is much used in maritime ethnography. While short and simple, it emphasises the admittedly important handing down of the methods and values of elders to the succeeding generation besides implying some unquestioning acceptance. However it lacks and even suggests the exclusion of the idea of any historically persistent (but possibly, over shorter periods of time, quite spasmodic) application of intelligence and conceptual ability toward improvements in design and technique without which change in ships, or for that matter anything else, would be hard to explain.

It follows from this somewhat philosophical discussion that any ship under study must be assumed (until proved otherwise) to have been successful in carrying out the functions expected of her within the limits acceptable in her own time and equally to represent, in all probability, a mature developed type. To be authentic, her reconstruction must be capable of the same performance, were it actually to be built and tested at sea. Any proposed reconstruction should therefore be analysed to see that it would:-

1. Be able to be built by the techniques and with the materials seen in the remains or known to be available in its time and region,

2. Float correctly and be adequately stable,

3. Be strong enough to withstand, for the duration of an adequate life, the loads imposed by cargo, waves at sea, impacts, by taking the ground and being hauled out of the water for repair,

4. Be propelled satisfactorily by the attested or assumed means in a controllable manner.

If the proposed reconstruction falls short in any of these fundamentals of what is known or could reasonably be supposed to be acceptable in her own time, its validity must be suspect, and, within the constraints of the evidence, it should be modified to rectify such shortfalls. It will be noticed that these aspects of a ship may have few and then only rather indirect effects upon details of shape and the more superficial aspects of appearance.

Such assessments call in principle for calculations of weight, displacement volume and the hydrostatic properties generally of the proposed reconstruction, of the centres of gravity of the ship in various conditions of loading, of her loading in such a way as to expose the bending and shearing actions upon her hull structure, and of quantities affecting manoeuvring and the stability of her steering when in motion. The necessary principles and methods to do all this have already been set out from the viewpoint of nautical archaeologists by McGrail (1987). They can also be studied in more detail in standard works on naval architecture.

The need for such calculations however depends in their particulars upon how much of the vessel is missing and has to be recreated to make a reconstruction and also upon the type of ship or craft in question. If she is of modest size, of portly beam and worked in sheltered waters, her design will have been shaped, in its fundamentals, for economic robustness more than by any drive towards limits of performance or seaworthiness. In building up a reconstruction of such a vessel from incomplete remains and any other evidence, the methods of naval architecture may have relatively little to contribute, though flotation, i.e. weight, displacement and stability, as well as strength must be seen to be satisfactory. In modest craft they are relatively easy to provide and so such craft enjoy more latitude in design and for the influences of tradition and taste springing from other aspects of culture, than more technically ambitious and extreme types of ship.

Accordingly, the dictates of the natural laws bear more harshly upon the design of ships of slender forms, lightly built or with fastenings of limited strength or stiffness. For them, the numerical assessments outlined here are not only more necessary to ensure the practicality of a proposed reconstruction, but they also narrow the range of choices open to the reconstructor in filling the gaps in the evidence. Indeed in the case of ships of extreme design, such as, for example, the ancient Greek trireme which verges on the limits of not only speed under oar, but of strength and of stability too, that range is reduced to virtually one choice as regards the fundamental design of that type of ship, given the presently known total of ancient evidence about it (Morrison and Coates 1980). The trireme is probably an extreme example of the extent to which naval architectural considerations can complete the definition of a reconstruction by supplementing ancient evidence. It was for that reason that the expense of actually building a trireme to prove its remarkable performance (or otherwise) and to learn something about operating large oared ships and hence about the bulk of naval warfare in history could be justified.

A reconstruction based without question upon measurements correctly obtained from a wreck may not be true of the ship in life if the wreck is deformed. A naval architectural analysis might reveal technical shortcomings in the reconstruction which could indicate deformations otherwise not suspected. Timber remains can become deformed owing to the disappearance of necessary parts of the hull structure causing it to approximate to a mechanism. For instance, remains of curved shell of the bottom often flatten out in the athwartships direction. If there was longitudinal curvature at the bilges, lateral flattening would tend to cause some rise of the ends (as may be demonstrated with the peel of a quarter of an orange), particularly as the ends might be unloaded by cargo and have some positive buoyancy, at least for a time, after submergence. In this way the original shape of the body of the hull could be misinterpreted from the remains, by, in such a case, giving the keel too great a rocker. On the other hand, a rockered bottom but one which is flat like that of a punt may tend to straighten with time, depending upon how it was supported after sinking or being abandoned (Wright 1990). A reconstruction which neglected to examine how the utility of the boat would be affected by varying degrees of rocker could be misleading. It is even possible that such an assessment could indicate mistakes

15

or omissions in recording.

Such application of naval architectural principles and methods is doing no more than giving the builders of the original the credit for a mature design of craft intelligently developed by long trial and error to optimise it for its function within the technical means available. That must surely be true of the vast majority of craft whose remains may be found today. The methods being discussed here may help us in trying to do as well in reconstructing them. Their builders deserve no less of us.

## References

McGrail, S. 1987. *Ancient Boats in North West Europe*. London: Longman.

Morrison, J.S., and Coates, J.F. 1986. *The Athenian Trireme*. Cambridge University Press.

Wright, E.V. 1990. *The Ferriby Boats. Seacraft of the Bronze Age*. London: Routledge.

**Plate 1.1**

*Pl. 1.1   The Hauterive-1976 logboat during excavation. Photo Eric Gentil.*

**Plate 1.2-1.3**

*Pl 1.2  Tool marks in the lime Auvernier-1973 logboat.*

*Pl 1.3  Cross section of the Männedorf-1977 logboat in one of the lifting frames used to extract it. Musée National, Zurich.*

**Plate 2.1-2.2**

*Pl. 2.1 Goldcliff, Wales 1992. Boat planks and roundwood forming Structure 1124 in grey clay. Photo M. Bell.*

*Pl. 2.2 Goldcliff, Wales 1991. The north-west corner of Building 1 showing post and wattle wall, roundwood floor and subdivisions (parallel with 1m rule). Photo Jonathan Parkhouse.*

**Plate 4.1-4.4**

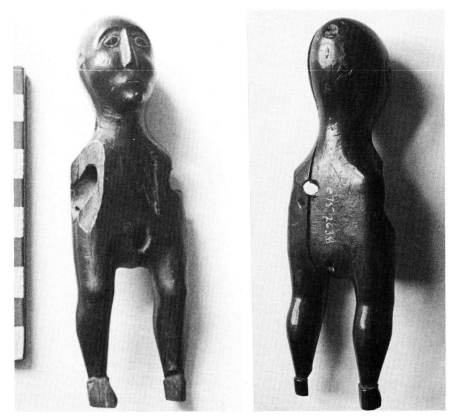

*Pl. 4.1-4.2 Strata Florida, front and back views. Photos B. J. Coles.*

*Pl. 4.3 Roos Carr, head of Figure 2.*
*Note indication of nostrils.*

*Pl. 4.4 Roos Carr, head of Figure 5.*
*Note remains of adhesive in eye socket*
*and mouth. Photos J. M. Coles.*

**Plate 4.5**

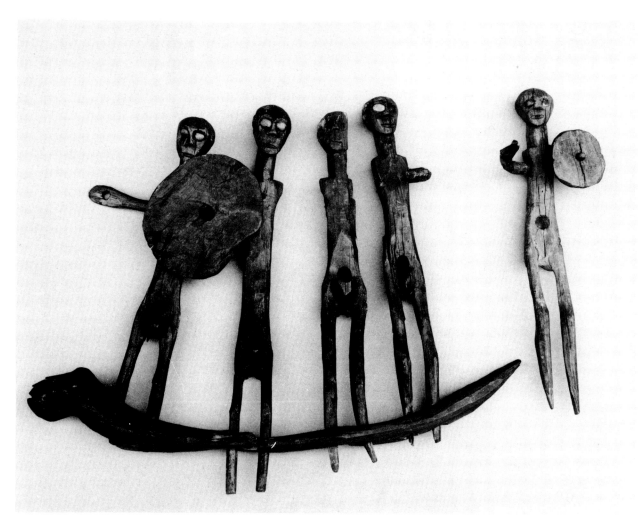

*Pl. 4.5  Roos Carr, the traditional view. The figures are numbered 1-5 from left to right. Photo Town Docks Museum, Hull.*

**Plate 5.1-5.2**

*Pl. 5.1 One boat or two? With hundreds of cupmarks, many more off the photo. Finntorp, Bohuslän, Sweden.*

*Pl. 5.2 A flotilla from Hornes, Østfold, Norway. Note the leaping man. Scale 1m. Photos the author.*

**Plate 5.3-5.4**

*Pl. 5.3 Sleek boat with helmsman/overseer and ? torch-bearing crew. The rock surface is constantly wet. Kasen Lövasen, Bohuslän, Sweden.*

*Pl. 5.4 Two ungainly boats, one with disc, the other with schematic acrobat. Part of a large panel from Hegre, Nord Trøndelag, Norway. Scale 25 cm. Photos the author.*

# Plate 6.1-6.2

*Pl. 6.1  Three-piece composite fishhook with attached double-looped spruce root string leader. Note base wrap (joining the two shanks) and barb wrap.*

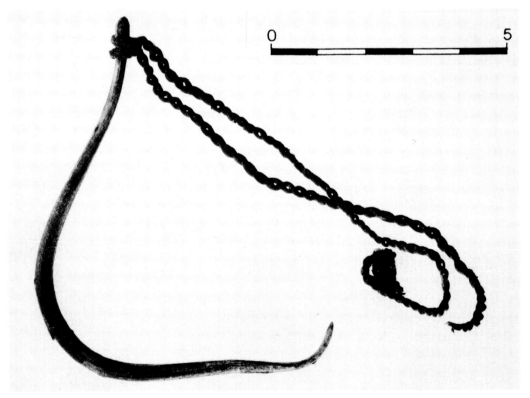

*Pl. 6.2  Bentwood fishhook with attached double-looped spruce root string leader. Note clove hitch joining leader to wooden hook. Scale cm.*

# 4

# ROOS CARR AND COMPANY

## *Bryony Coles*

The Roos Carr figures are well-known, human-like wooden carvings with quartz eyes staring out from poster or book cover, expression blank or enigmatic depending on the views of the beholder. Roos Carr, the place, lies a short distance inland from the Humber and the figures were found here *c* 1836, in a ditch which is thought once to have been a tidal creek leading to the Humber. But it is not only their find-spot which brings these carvings within the orbit of Ted Wright's Humber fieldwork: the five surviving people have a fine, animal-headed wooden boat at their disposal.

A few years ago, the available information relating to Roos Carr and to other wooden anthropomorphic figures from Britain and Ireland was brought together, along with AMS radiocarbon dates obtained from samples of wood taken from the figures themselves (Coles 1990). Whether or not this exercise left the figures any less enigmatic, it did indicate that all those studied were prehistoric in origin, ranging in date from the later Neolithic to the Iron Age, and a certain similarity of style and purpose was suggested. Since then, several other wooden figures have been drawn to my attention, and a preliminary account of these will be given here, along with some further consideration of the Roos Carr ensemble.

First, the 'new' wooden figures. There are four of these, two extant and two known only from nineteenth century references. None of the four is securely dated, but either the context of their discovery or their appearance, or both, suggest in each case that the figure may have some affinity with the dated prehistoric examples discussed previously. The two which are probably now lost come from Oakhanger Mosses near Crewe and from the peats between Misson and Haxey just off the Isle of Axholme. Of the surviving two, one comes from Ickham near Canterbury and the other from Strata Florida north of Tregaron (fig. 4.1).

### Oakhanger

The reference to the Oakhanger discovery was sent to me by Mrs C. Micklewright of Haslington near Crewe, whose letter I quote:

> The following passage occurs in a publication of 1856, "Barthomley" by the Rev. Edward Hinchliffe one-time rector of the parish of Barthomley as part of his description of a parishioner, Daniel Stringer, then deceased.
>
> "He was digging, when a young man, in one of the Oakhanger mosses, and, at a great depth, hit upon a wooden figure, rude and grotesque, but complete with eyes, nose and mouth. He concluded it to be an *idol,* and sent it to the British Museum with an account of its discovery, but never learnt whether it arrived safe there."
>
> Sadly, the object is not at the Museum and there is no correspondence about the find in the archives....

Hinchliffe had made reference to Daniel Stringer earlier on, in his account of Barthomley, noting that Stringer was born in 1743. Therefore, if he found the 'idol' when he was a young man, this could have been between about 1760 and 1780, if one allows that a man who lived to be 99, as Stringer did, might in retrospect extend his youth into other people's middle age.

On reading of the discovery, it seemed to me odd for a young peat-digger to decide that a wooden figure properly belonged in the British Museum. However, Hinchliffe's description of Stringer, leading up to the passage quoted above, suggests that he had both initiative and intelligence:

> "Daniel Stringer was another worthy of this township... He attained the great age of 99 years; all his faculties being sound to the very last. He was a man, both in talent and information, far in advance of his

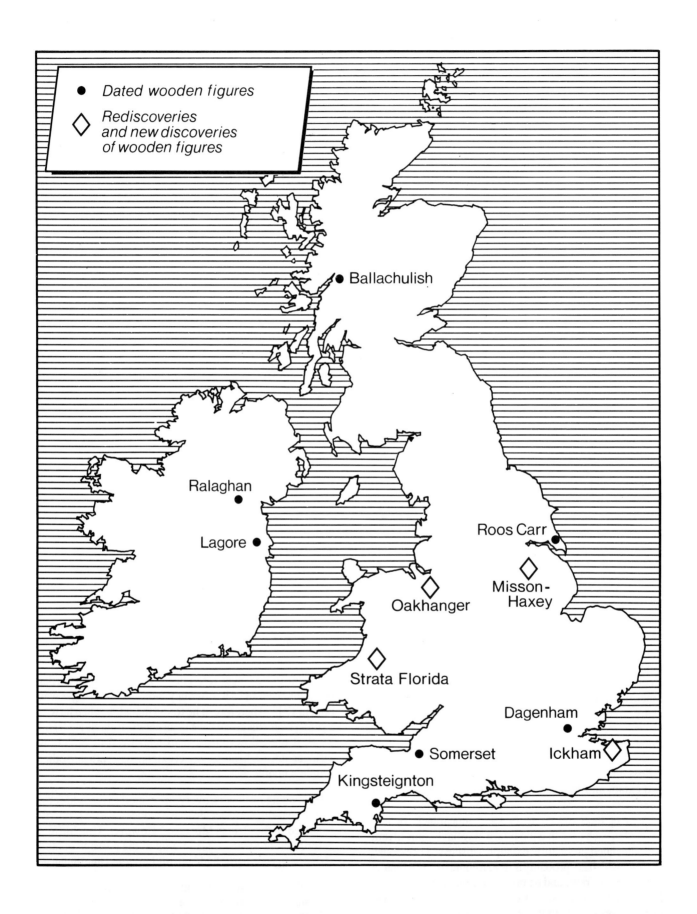

*Fig. 4.1 Discoveries of wooden anthropomorphic figures from Britain and Ireland.*

own class, and only wanted education and opportunity to become a distinguished character. He was a tall, fine-built fellow, and, in youth, must have been extremely good-looking. He was a miller and small farmer; and, sometimes, stole a few sly hours from his business, to perpetrate a little poaching. One of his hands bore a fearful mark of his propensity. A long time ago, the land about Manneley Mere, for many acres, was covered with rushes and high sedges, and was, of course, a favourite resort of wild fowl. Here Daniel used to have a little clandestine sport; and once, when there in search of it, a flock of wild-geese rose with loud screams before him; he fired, the gun burst in his hand, and shattered several of his fingers. His observation of passing events and social progress was uncommonly acute: nothing seemed to have escaped him, and this made his conversation both interesting and instructive. "I went", said he to me, " with many others to stare and wonder at the making of the new-cut (the canal), and what a great and useful undertaking we thought it, never to be beaten by any other; but I have lived to see the making and opening of a railway, which beats all that has ever been done yet. I expect it will make a great change wherever it goes." His mind penetrated beyond the mere surface of the work, and already foresaw, what people in his class would little think of, the gigantic strides which civilization would take by its help, even in the most retired and backward spots of England."

*(Hinchliffe 1856, 116-117)*

All that Hinchliffe writes of Stringer adds credence to the account of the Oakhanger Mosses 'idol' and its despatch to the British Museum. Like Stringer, we do not know if it reached its destination as nothing more has been heard of it. Could it lurk in some forgotten corner? It seems not. On the basis of the information available I would accept the Oakhanger figure as genuine, and possibly the first wooden anthropomorphic carving to be recognised as an antiquity: the discovery took place half a century or more before the Roos Carr figures were found in 1836. The brief description of where the Oakhanger figure was found, in the mosses and well below the surface, sounds not unlike the context of discovery of the Ballachulish or Ralaghan carvings, and 'a wooden figure, rude and grotesque, but complete with eyes, nose and mouth' could refer to either Ballachulish or Ralaghan or any of the Roos Carr figures, all of which have eyes and nose and mouth. The dated figures with definite mouths all belong to the first half of the 1st millennium BC, those which are older or younger having a rudimentary mouth or no mouth at all.

## Misson-Haxey

The account of the Misson-Haxey discovery was provided by Rick Turner of CADW, as follows:

I promised you information concerning another wooden idol from peat. On rereading the reference it may not be relevant but this is it. Peck, W. 1815 *A Topographical Account of the Isle of Axholme* Vol. I, 8, (Doncaster):

"In August 1802, a statue of oak, black as ebony, about two yards high and carved in the habit of a Roman Warrior, was found several feet deep, between Misson and Haxey; one hand held an arrow and a bow was slung over the shoulder. This account I received from a person who saw it exhibited; another informed me there was an inscription, which I have not been able to procure. The statue was claimed by a variety of workmen who were digging at the time and in consequence of passing through many of their hands is now become mutilated".

This suggests the genuine discovery of a wooden figure deposited in wet conditions where peat formed. The details indicate a carving which differs from the prehistoric examples from Britain and Ireland principally through being clothed. There are, however, clothed figures of late prehistoric date from the continent, for example the massive wooden figure from Geneva which has been dated by dendrochronology to the final century BC (Mottier 1976 in Deyts 1983, 178-179). If we take Peck's account at face value and assume the figure was 'carved in the habit of a Roman warrior', deposition in the early centuries AD would be most likely. The peats around the Isle of Axholme have yielded various objects over the centuries, having been drained and 'improved' over many generations. Among these are several bog bodies (Briggs and Turner 1986, 186-187). It is just possible that the life-size Misson-Haxey figure was deposited in the course of activities similar to, or connected with, the deposition of bog bodies, as suggested previously for the Ballachulish figure (Coles 1990, 331).

## Strata Florida

Much of the information about the third 'new' discovery, including its present location, has also been provided by Rick Turner. The figure in question was published in *Archaeologia Cambrensis* for 1903 (vol. III, 6th series, 284-286) as follows:

"WOODEN FIGURE FOUND AT STRATA FLORIDA, CARDIGANSHIRE - the remarkable carved wooden figure here illustrated belongs to the Rev. D.L.Davies, Vicar of Talgarth, and was exhibited by him when the Association visited his church during the Brecon Meeting in 1902. It is stated to have been found at Strata Florida, Cardiganshire. Mr. C.H.Read, F.S.A., of the British Museum, to whom the figure has been shown, expresses an opinion that it is of foreign origin, probably North American."

The figure was illustrated with front- and side-view photographs that show a dumpy battered body with a large head and carefully shaped legs and feet but no arms. The overall effect of the carving has some similarities to both Kingsteignton and Lagore (Coles 1990 figs. 7 and 9), although the Strata Florida figure is distinguished by its shiny surface. It was this last characteristic perhaps which suggested a North American origin to Read.

Strata Florida, the Valley of the Flowers, consists now of the ruins of a once-fine Cistercian abbey, built beside

Afon Teifi. At first sight, this would appear to be where the figure was discovered and the valley of the Teifi at this point provides possible, although not ideal, conditions for the deposition and survival of a wooden object in undisturbed wet conditions. Some distance downstream, however, Afon Teifi flows into the Tregaron complex of raised bogs and here, just on the northern edge, was built Strata Florida railway station in the mid-nineteenth century. Peat cutting took place around the edges of the bog and the Manchester to Milford Haven railway line was laid across it, both activities giving opportunity for discovery of the wooden figure. Strata Florida railway station provides an altogether more likely context than the abbey (and, in its own way, no less romantic): an active peatbog was a suitable location for deposition, as for Ballachulish and Ralaghan and possibly Oakhanger, and the bog would be an ideal medium for the long-term preservation of the carving.

The area of bog immediately by Strata Florida railway station is known as Gors Dol-fawr and here, in 1891, a bog body was found (Turner *pers. comm.*; Briggs and Turner 1986, 187 no.48). Tanned skin and bones survived of an apparently decapitated man; the remains were subsequently buried in the neighbouring churchyard of Ystrad Meurig. The possible affinity of the Ballachulish and Misson-Haxey figures with bog bodies has been noted above. If the Strata Florida figure is genuine, deposited in antiquity in Gors Dol-fawr, and if the body found there in 1811 was also deposited in antiquity, and in some way ritual given its decapitated condition, there is then some strengthening of the tenuous link between wooden anthropomorphic figures and bog bodies.

But is the figure genuine? It is now held at Carmarthen Museum where it was found in the stores in the 1970s, with no documentation to show when or how it was acquired by the Museum (Chris Delaney *pers. comm.*) but it is undoubtedly the same carving as that illustrated in *Archaeologia Cambrensis*. At first sight (pl.4.1, 4.2), the figure appears tiny, highly polished and with a delicate, expressive face compared to the previously-studied carvings. On closer examination, various similarities to the known prehistoric group become more apparent. At the time of writing, it is not possible to say if the Strata Florida figure is a British antiquity or an ethnographic import, but it is sufficiently intriguing to warrant a brief description and discussion of the possibilities.

The carving stands 129mm high, 40mm maximum width at the hips, 32mm from front to back of head and 18mm from front to back of hips. It was made from a half or two thirds stem of roundwood with pith that can be traced from top back of head and down the centre left of the trunk to the left groin. The flat back of the figure may be a split radial surface but the front flatness of the trunk was achieved by carving. Growth rings can be seen on the head and left cheek in particular, various small knots indicate the position of side branches, and one branch looks to have been trimmed off the top of the head. Small facets and knife marks are evident under the chin and on

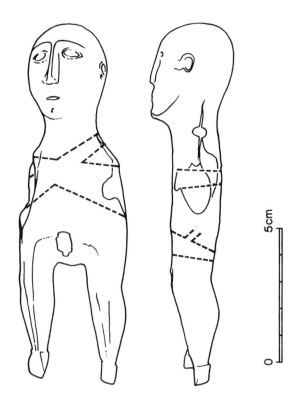

*Fig. 4.2 Sketch of Strata Florida figure to illustrate arrangement of holes.*

the shoulders and groin and around the openings of various holes made through the body. The head and legs have smooth, highly finished surfaces in contrast to the trunk.

The condition of the carving is generally good, although there is a bad split down the left centre back, near the pith, and there has been damage to both shoulders. Since 1903, when the right foot was already missing, the left foot has been lost as well and the surface exposed is rougher and less polished that the other surfaces exposed by damage (e.g. right foot, left shoulder hole), suggesting that these other areas of damage occurred before discovery, or that the wood was treated in some way before the left foot was lost.

The Strata Florida figure has a large head relative to its body, three-dimensional and relatively naturalistic with carefully-carved eyes, nose with nostrils, ears, mouth and chin. The armless trunk, by contrast, is a slab or rectangle of wood lacking human features and distinguished chiefly by the complicated arrangement of holes drilled through it. From part-way down each side of the trunk a hole passes diagonally through the body to exit at the side of the neck, and these two holes must cross each other. Another hole passes from front to back of the left shoulder, intersecting with the left diagonal hole, and rising from front to back. A fourth, pubic hole slants down through the body to exit at the back just above the base of the trunk, and a few millimetres in from the front of this pubic hole a further hole has been drilled through its roof up into the core of the trunk. Fig. 4.2 attempts to illustrate the disposition of these holes.

There is a small metal pin at the lower end of the right shoulder hole, which may or may not be contemporary with the carving, and what are probably small drilled holes on the front and back of the trunk near the left shoulder may have been made for similar pins, with the remnant of a pin possibly surviving on the front.

The legs, like the head, are three-dimensional and carefully executed, and a ridge around the ankle suggests the feet may have been carved as shod but they are now too damaged to be sure.

Although the naturalistic head of this figure distinguishes it from the Roos Carr group, it could be argued that it is no more different than Lagore with its featureless face. There is some similarity in a) the general idea of detail for head and legs but not for trunk, b) an armless trunk with holes, and c) a pubic hole but no obvious indication of the intended sex of the figure.

The presence of the metal pin, incidentally, does not rule out a prehistoric origin since the bulk of dated figures were carved after metal came into use in north-western Europe. The pin could be contemporary with the carving, or it could be modern, inserted after discovery.

Two steps could be taken to illuminate the origin of the carving, sampling it for identification of the wood species and sampling it for AMS dating. Neither is really justified until the possible ethnographic sources have been more fully investigated. So far, no ethnographer has made a positive identification of the style of carving. One intriguing possibility is that the figure is indeed North American in origin, as Read suggested, but of some antiquity and an early import to Wales during the active monastic life of Strata Florida abbey. As for prehistoric analogies, there are resemblances to the figures on the Gundestrup cauldron and to various of the small bronze figures of northern Europe.

## Ickham

The fourth find (fig.4.3) comes from a site near Ickham in Kent. It was drawn to my attention by John Price of the Ancient Monuments Laboratory. Peter Clark of the Canterbury Archaeological Trust (who has recently taken on responsibility for the publication of the site) has informed me that the figure was found, unstratified, with material that was predominantly late Roman in date - but all of the material has still to be studied, and no conclusions should be drawn as yet regarding the date or the context of the wooden figure.

The figure was carved out of maple wood (ident. Jacqui Watson, Ancient Monuments Laboratory), apparently from roundwood. It survives at *c*. 325 mm high, about the size of Kingsteignton or the Roos Carr figures. It has stick-like arms in the Ballachulish style, although with more pronounced shoulders. The legs were apparently splayed, more akin to Broddenbjerg (Coles 1990, pl.31b) than to any of the British or Irish examples. The lower torso is too damaged to identify the intended sex of the figure unless, and again like Broddenbjerg, the 'leg' is a penis.

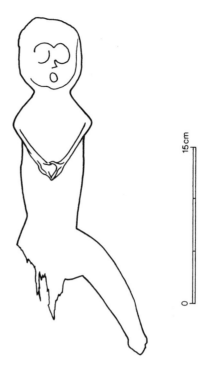

*Fig. 4.3 Sketch of Ickham figure.*

## Roos Carr

The five Roos Carr figures and boat are currently (summer 1993) undergoing treatment at Doncaster Museum's Conservation Laboratory, where I have been able to examine them thanks to Helen Cox, Conservator, and Andrew Foxon, Curator of Archaeology at Hull City Museum where the figures usually reside. The main objective of the conservation exercise is to prevent any further deterioration of the carvings, but it seems likely that in the process something will be learnt of earlier attempts at conservation and manipulation of the figures for museum display, and new information may emerge about the original carving and putting-together of the pieces. The Figures (pl.4.5) are numbered here as in Coles 1990, from 1 on the left to 5 on the right.

At the time of writing, the work is at an early stage but already Dr Allan Hall (York Environmental Archaeology Unit) has identified the wood of Figure 1 as yew not pine, and as all the original wood has the same outward appearance it is likely that yew was used throughout. It was previously suggested (Coles 1990) that the Figures had been wrongly assembled, and this now seems all the more likely. Figures 1 and 2 share certain features which are not found on Figures 3, 4 and 5, such as nostrils (pl.4.3). Figures 3, 4 and 5 all have legs which are pointed at the end and which have a calf bulge below the knee whereas Figures 1 and 2 have straighter legs, probably originally cut square across the end for Figure 2 but recently cut across for Figure 1 so that one cannot tell what the original end was like. Comparing the legs of the Figures with the spacing of the boat holes, it seems likely that Figures 3, 4 and 5 were the original crew, along with another Figure now missing, and Figures 1 and 2 belonged to a separate ensemble. Figure 3 would fit at the head end of the boat, facing in the opposite direction to the way Figure 1 was forced into it for display, and Figure 5 would fit at the tail end, with Figure 4 somewhere in between (the foot-holes are fairly heavily damaged and repaired in the middle of the boat, and it may not prove possible to determine whether Figure 4 belongs nearer the head or the tail).

Figure 5, the one which came much later to Hull Museum than the others, has the remains of a thin layer of what is probably adhesive in its empty left eye socket, and a small amount of similar looking material in its mouth (pl.4.4). Helen Cox's present work may determine whether this is ancient or modern. If the former, there is a possibility that Figure 5 at least had a mouth inlay (white ?) as well as stones for eyes.

Most of the Figures have liberal amounts of red sealing-wax-like material, especially around the arm-holes, and this is more likely to be recent than ancient, as is the adhesive used to mend arms and legs and boat-base. There are also rather more modern nails inserted into the Figures than was previously noted. Full details should be available once the present treatment is completed.

## Discussion

It is promising that further finds of wooden figures have come to light in recent years. Even if it is too early, or information is too scanty, to be sure of their provenance and date, the range of prehistoric anthropomorphic wooden carvings seems likely to be extended, and I am all the more convinced that there are other figures, thought of as 'old dolls' or, more likely, as ethnographic imports, which closer examination would show to be probably indigenous and prehistoric. There will always be a problem with ancient wood used in recent times for carving, but it should usually be possible to distinguish carving carried out on green wood from that carried out on bog-oak or its equivalent.

As for the purpose or purposes of the carvings, I have previously made some guarded suggestions (Coles 1990, 332). A slightly different light is perhaps thrown by the following quotation:

> Bor's sons [Odin, Vili and Ve ...] were walking by the sea-shore, and came upon two logs. They plucked them up and shaped them into human beings. The first gave them breath and life, the second understanding and motion, the third form, speech, hearing and sight ... From them descended the races of Men...
>
> (Snorri's *Prose Edda*, trans. R.I. Page 1990).

There is a certain attraction in the possibility that Roos Carr and company show us how our prehistoric predecessors visualised their own forebears.

## References

Briggs, C.S. and Turner, R.W. 1986. A Gazetteer of Bog Burials from Britain and Ireland. In I.M.Stead, J.B. Bourke and Don Brothwell (eds), *Lindow Man: The Body in the Bog*, 181-195. London: British Museum Publications.

Coles, Bryony 1990. Anthropomorphic Wooden Figures from Britain and Ireland. *Proceedings of the Prehistoric Society* 56, 315-333.

Deyts, S. 1983. *Les Bois Sculptés des Sources de la Seine.* XLII supplément à Gallia. Paris: Editions du CNRS.

Hinchliffe, Rev. Edward 1856. *Barthomley: in Letters from a former Rector to his Eldest Son*, Newcastle-under-Lyme.

Page, R.I. 1990. *Norse Myths*. London: British Museum Publications.

Peck, W. 1815. *A Topographical Account of the Isle of Axholme*. Vol. I. Doncaster.

# 5

# BOATS ON THE ROCKS

## *John Coles*

The discovery of the Dover boat, preceded by the several sewn-plank fragments from Caldicot and Goldcliff, has focussed attention once again on the magisterial work of Ted Wright on his Ferriby boats (1990). All these finds have established the sewn-plank boats of Ferriby tradition as the major craft of Bronze Age Britain. This is not to downgrade the local importance of the ubiquitous logboats but I think there is a fundamental dissimilarity between plank-built boats and 'dugouts' in terms of the requirements of craftmanship, carrying capacities and 'worthiness' of the boats for the communities concerned. The wholly unexpected discovery at Dover, and the plank debris at the two Welsh sites, suggest the widespread adoption and existence of plank boats, and more finds can be expected as intertidal foreshore and river valley surveys, and watching briefs, are conducted. Deep holes in the centre of coastal towns were a less likely source - until Dover.

Britain by the mid-second millennium BC was well-insulated by sea from the continental mainland. A long coastline, many western islands, and major river systems such as the Severn, Thames, Trent, Tyne and Clyde all contributed to the need for watercraft other than logboats for traffic along and across protected waters. Large load carriers, wide-bottomed for bulky cargo including animals, propelled by pole or paddle, were an obvious necessity for communities engaged in local transport and also in exchanges and trade within Britain; perhaps there was an occasional foray across wider waters - to Ireland and to the mainland of Europe. Cultural material and shared traditions seem to speak of both inner and outer contact zones throughout the Bronze Age.

One other area in north-western Europe was equally dependent upon water transport in the Bronze Age. In southern Scandinavia, from North Sea Rogaland east to Uppland and south to Bornholm in the Baltic Sea, the Bronze Age landscape was inseparable from the sea. In the last 8000 years or so, uplift of the land through isostatic

recovery has gradually widened the landmass, exposed new islands, created peninsulas and drawn water from once-drowned river valleys. In the Bronze Age (*c.* 1500-*c.* 500 BC), the sea still covered many areas of southern Scandinavia, and mapping these landscapes shows considerable variation from those of today. In certain areas, land now at 20m altitude lay on the coastline, in other regions the sea level was at the 10 or 15m present contour, and in yet other areas there has been little or no land uplift and today's shore was a Bronze Age shore. As much of southern Scandinavia is rather flat, with low hills only, even slight differences in the land-sea relationship drowned, or exposed, substantial areas. In the second and early first millennia BC the sea was a dominant feature but was slowly withdrawing as the land rose. This gradual uplift of the land created new shorelines even within the short period of the classic Bronze Age, and old shorelines became dry and upslope.

Today, many parts of southern Scandinavia are linked by boat, and ferry crossings are as numerous as the bridges thrown over narrow straits; during a two-week journey in south-west Norway in 1990, I had 13 ferry crossings of one sort or another, and crossed innumerable bridges. In the Bronze Age, there was an even greater need for short-haul and long-haul transport by water. Christensen rightly points to the great variety of more recent boats created for work all along the Norwegian coasts (1988), surely a reflection of the importance of the sea and the ability of people to invent and adapt suitable craft for all occasions.

The evidence for ancient local and long-distance travel, across narrow straits and across the North Sea and the Baltic, exists in the variable and always incomplete archaeological record. The bare record consists of materials, artifacts, settlements, burials and the like. It excludes factors such as natural human curiosity to explore, particularly over water. And it combines elements at different levels of intensity and performance. On the one hand are the basic raw materials of the archaeological Bronze Age,

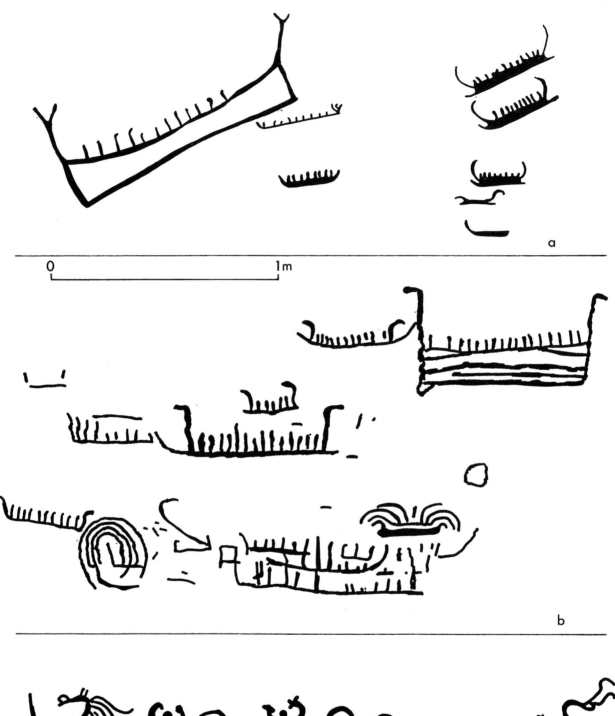

Fig. 5.1 a. Part of boat panel from Hakeröd, Bohuslän, Sweden; b. Part of a large panel with simple boat lines from Åmøy, Rogaland, Norway; c. Huge boat with elaborate features from Bakkehaugen, Østfold, Norway. All to same scale. Sources: a. Fredsjö 1981; b. Fett and Fett 1941; c. Hagen 1990.

copper and tin, gold and stone, some brought from long distances. Barely visible are other materials such as furs, fish and humans, parts of both local and wider relations. And wood, that paramount necessity for almost all non-industrial communities, was likely to be widely available, carefully managed, and particular species and individual stands prized and protected. Wood for houses and barns, and for other important elements of social life, from totem-poles to coffins, furniture to drinking cups, was in demand, and none greater than for transportation by wheeled vehicle or by boat. Archaeologists often speak of the wider connections of the Bronze Age, but purely local needs - burial of the dead on off-shore islands, seasonal seafaring activities and movement of supplies over short distances - suggest that boats of several different kinds were a normal part of life's necessities in the landscape of Bronze Age and Early Iron Age Scandinavia.

The record of the craft that carried goods and gifts, the living and the dead, and opened new areas for settlement, is very poor. There are many logboats from many parts of north-western Europe, dating from the Mesolithic onwards, but of plank-built boats there is little in southern Scandinavia before the closing centuries BC. The Hjortspring boat, of the third century BC, tantalises us by its craftmanship and technical sophistication, suggesting an earlier period when such plank-built boats were being developed (Rosenberg 1937). So we have two pressing reasons to look for evidence of the existence of traditional and successful boats in the region during the Bronze Age: 1) the presumed earlier phases leading to the Hjortspring craft; 2) the evidence for Bronze Age travel and transport. Both of these needs are satisfied by an unusual source of archaeological evidence to which I now turn.

The major source of information about water-based activities in the south Scandinavian Bronze Age lies in the rock carvings that adorn many hundreds of sites in a wide sweep from Trøndelag and Rogaland (in north and west) to Uppland and Småland (in east) and Skåne and Bornholm (in south). Central areas of this huge territory, Østfold and Bohuslän, and Östergötland, have many hundreds of carved sites and many thousands of images. Within the variety of subjects selected for expression by the Bronze Age artists are boat-like designs, which are the most numerous of all images except for the ubiquitous cupmarks (pl.5.1). This interest in the representation of boats is also evident in the boat-shaped burial monuments of the later Bronze Age (Müller-Wille 1968-69). The boat-settings, often containing cremation burials, consist of lines of upright stones, tallest at the ends, lowest at the middle, forming elegant double-prowed representations.

Carving designs into solid rock is no easy task and the canvas itself suppresses the amount of detail that can be conveyed; this suggest that any and all elements depicted were meant to be there, and no fripperies are likely to be present. Because most of the carvings are on living rock, the images are in their original place and, unlike bronze implements, could not be transported to foreign contexts.

In addition, many of the other images carved on the rocks are represented in the real world of material culture; waggons, wheels, shields, axes, lurer, animals such as oxen, horse, deer and dog, are present in the archaeological record, and the carvings also depict the humans who presumably had important roles in acquiring, using and distributing this material. Therefore there seems no reason to doubt, except for the sake of pure b.m. argument, that the carvings of boat-like designs represent real once-existing boats even if some were distorted or exaggerated for symbolic reasons. The problem, or one problem, is to identify the kind of boat represented in the carvings.

It will be obvious that this is not a new question; it has already been pursued by a number of archaeologists. Many of the presumed boat designs have keel line, gunwale, end-lines joining the two (e.g. fig.5.1a left), open or lined (e.g. fig.5.2m) or hammered-out hull (e.g. fig.5.2f), prow and other terminals, crew strokes and other cargo. I deliberately use the terms employed by the archaeologists who have presented analyses of the boat elements (e.g. Marstrander 1963; Malmer 1981; Burenhult 1980). Some designs are much more simple than this. Variation exists in the way the basic shape was represented, and one author has proposed a scheme with 99 different versions; he says "the flexibility of the system also makes it easier to memorize the characteristics of the 99 types" (Malmer 1981). I know of no one who has made the slightest effort so to do. Of greater interest is the representation of crew and cargo; simple strokes may indicate humans (fig.5.1a-b), and sometimes cupmarks on the stroke-tops suggest heads (fig.5.3c). Some crew are better-defined, with waving arms, or two legs and a proper body (fig.5.1c), and some carry curved objects, perhaps lurer (fig.5.3f), or they brandish other things (pl.5.3). Occasionally a human is shown jumping into or doing a back-flip over a boat, and a disc may hover above the hull (pl.5.2, 5.4; fig.5.2b). In a few cases a crew of simple strokes is controlled by human figures at fore and/ or aft, carved more deeply, and impressive in size (pl.5.3).

The boats themselves range from under 20cm (fig.5.2g) to well over 2m in length (fig.5.1c; all the drawings are at the same scale), and they have been studied by a number of archaeological boat-persons. I cannot propose any new classification of boats here, or anywhere, and will only comment that I have probably seen and recorded over 4000 boats on rocks from all the main areas of carvings in Scandinavia, sufficient to know that there are strong regional shapes and, more importantly, to think that these need not represent only one standard type of boat.

The main debate about the boat designs is between the hiders and the plankers. Do these carvings show hide boats of strong north Eurasian tradition or do they represent plank-built craft? If the latter, was the type developed within Scandinavia or was it an idea brought from the Mediterranean? There is considerable disagreement on these issues. All authorities seem to agree, however, that rafts and logboats are excluded from the

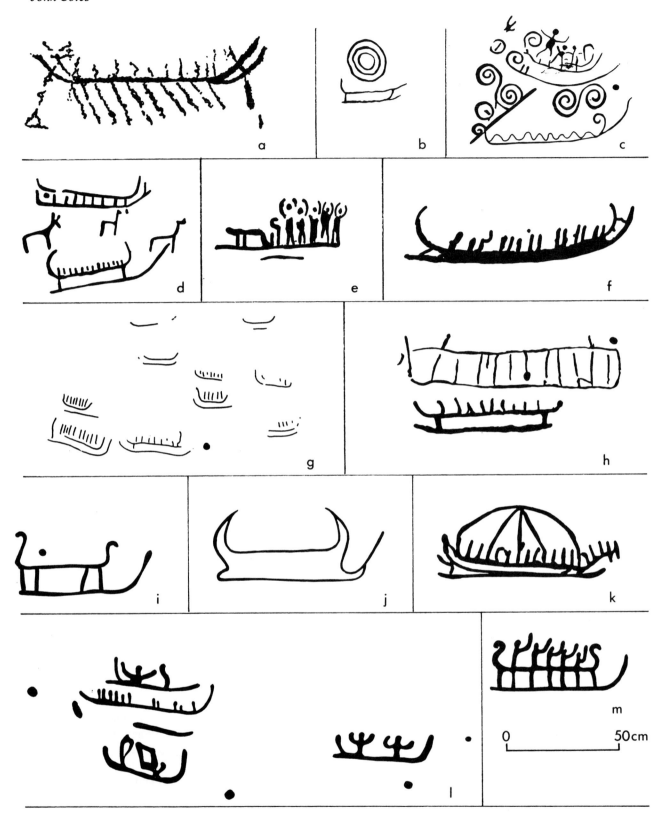

Fig. 5.2 a. Boat with oars and steering oars from Dalbo, Akershus, Norway; b. Tiny boat with disc suspended from Hällby, Litslena, Uppland; c. Spiral complex with simple boat lines from Dammen, Tjörn, Sweden; d. Sledge-like 'boats' from Hakeröd, Bohuslän, Sweden; e. Raft with figures from Hamm, Bohuslän, Sweden; f. Long boat with paired crew from Niels Juelsgate, Oslo; g. Small single and double line boats from Galov, Tjörn, Sweden; h. Boat and enigmatic image (boat, map, house?) from Boda, Uppland, Sweden; i. Sledge from Kalnes, Østfold, Norway; j. Boat, perhaps hide boat, from Enköping Vårfrukyrka, Uppland, Sweden; k. Boat with sail lines from Järrestad, Scania, Sweden; l. Simple boats, perhaps logboats, from Nordom, Østfold, Norway; m. Boat, perhaps hide boat, from Kalnes, Østfold, Norway. All to same scale.
Sources: a. Østmo 1992; f. Østmo 1990; d.-e. Fredsjö 1981; k. Burenhult 1971-72; all others Coles unpub.

debate, because of their relative simplicity and the complexity of the carved images especially the high posts at bow and stern. There also seems to be broad agreement on chronology - that the period of carvings is *c.* 1500 - *c.* 300 BC or beyond, from the earliest Bronze Age of the north and well into the Early Iron Age. This time-frame encompasses the Ferriby and Dover boats, just about, also perhaps the Caldicot and Goldcliff fragments, and the Hjortspring boat. It also neatly allows a chronological connection with certain Mediterranean boats depicted in the art and designs of that region.

Various authorities have advanced theories on the type of boat represented in the carvings. Marstrander made an experimental construction of a hide boat, using one of the Kalnes carvings (fig.5.2m) as a model (1963; Johnstone 1972), and he argued for an independent Nordic development of a hide boat capable of sea voyages by paddlers - there was no sail. Marstrander's views were accepted by Glob (1969), at least for the independence of the tradition. Burenhult, in an elaborate classification, suggested that "occasionally extremely intensive contact with the Mediterranean world" over a period of 3500 years had contributed to the appearance of the Scandinavian boats (1980), but such intensities are not laid out and I doubt they can be. Malmer, creating his 99 types of boat representation, advanced the argument for Mediterranean contact and inspiration (1981), although he skates over the general absence of Mediterranean types of boat propulsion on the Scandinavian carvings. Boats of the second millennium BC in the Mediterranean were normally propelled by rowing or sailing, but there is little sign of either method in the carvings of the north. Of the thousands of carvings of boats, perhaps 15 have mast-lines (fig.5.3d) (Burenhult 1971-72) and barely any have a sail clearly shown (fig.5.2k).

The technical discussion was pursued by Hale, himself an oarsman, who tried to shred the hide boat idea in a single sentence: the art shows a "one-piece keel or bottom plank from which rise the stem, stern-post and ribs and which itself extends beyond the stem to form the prominent beak"; a skin boat could not possibly have these features (1980). Doubtless there are those who could argue against this view. Few authorities have spent much time on propulsion - there are a few carvings of boats with steering oars or paddles shown, some quite explicitly (fig.5.3a; pl.5.2), and the huge and well-known Brandskogen boat has a row of paddlers, but these are exceptional. At Dalbo, at the top of the Oslofjord, a series of rather worn carvings includes one boat which appears to be rowed rather than paddled (fig.5.2a) (Østmo 1992), and a number of other carvings show boats with crew, variable in number but in distinct pairs - perhaps an attempt to show side-by-side paddlers or rowers (fig.5.2f). But a huge majority of the boats move without effort through the water, without paddle, oar, rudder or sail. Indeed, there is no sign of the water itself. The boats seem not to be part-submerged - they are supported on an invisible medium, suspended in a void.

In all the thoughts expressed about the boats there are some entrenched positions, and boat carving archaeology is clearly an emotive experience. With as many as 99 (theoretical) different ways by which a boat could be shown, or even 57 varieties, there may be rafts, logboats, hide boats and plank boats all represented; no steamboats have been identified. From my observations of boat-like carvings (and my profound ignorance about the finer points of boat features and terminology) it seems to me that the carvings are precise, explicit, and varied enough to suggest that they represent specific varieties with different features.

We know that Bronze Age people of north-western Europe had communication over water, had wide contacts, had heavy and cumbersome materials to transport, had extensive timber stands and fine wood technologies to exploit and develop, and had actual rafts, logboats, plank-built boats and, probably, hide boats in certain areas. They also had skis and sledges. Other important artifacts and possessions of cultural significance were depicted on the rocks of Scandinavia, many of these objects involving elaborate technology, exotic materials and long-established traditions. Where Bronze Age settlement was extensive, the land fertile, the sea bounteous, and where communication by land was difficult, the boat carvings are often present. Rogaland in south-west Norway is dependent on the sea for outside contacts, and it has many boat carvings. Conversely, there are few boat carvings in Jutland, an area with direct land links to the south in this case. Dalsland in western Sweden, an inland province, has complex rock carvings in which boats do not figure largely. Where sea transport was important and rock carving traditions existed, boats were depicted, and I suggest that all kinds of watercraft were needed and were recorded in stone. These were:

1. Even a raft is an investment in time, energy and resources. "Attempts which have been made to interpret the ships in the rock carvings as rafts are not convincing" (Marstrander 1963). Yet not all carvings of possible boats have upturned prow and stern, and single lines with crew might represent simple rafts - an ideal bulk carrier for inland waters, across streams, down rivers, over still ponds and shallow lakes; there is ample historic evidence for the successful use of rafts in all these situations. (fig.5.2e might be a raft but it is carved upside down on the rock, judged by the other carvings at Hamm).

2. A logboat is a considerable undertaking and the abundance of such objects in lake muds and peat bogs shows its common value. "It is pre-eminently the boat of the primitive jungle" (Marstrander 1963); the concept of a Scandinavian jungle is interesting to contemplate. But for inland waters and calmer seas the logboat was useful, and perhaps the simplest 'boat lines' on the rocks represent these river craft (fig.5.1b, 5.2l, 5.3e: the little boat in

27

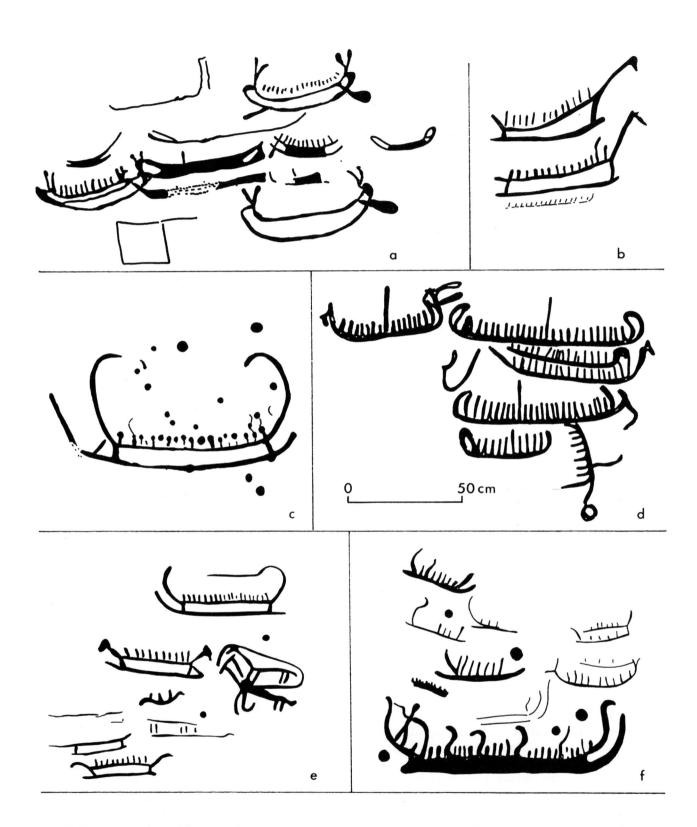

*Fig. 5.3 a. Major part of panel of boats with steering oars from Bjorngård, Nord-Trøndelag, Norway; b. Unlikely boats from Hällby, Uppland, Sweden; c. Boat with exaggerated lines from Biskopskula, Uppland, Sweden; d. Part of panel of boats with mast-like lines from Hästhallen, Blekinge, Sweden; e. Small part of panel of many boats from Boglösa, Uppland, Sweden; f. Part of boat panel from Y. Gånsta, Uppland, Sweden. All to same scale.*
*Sources: a. Sognnes 1987 and Coles; d. Burenhult 1971-72; all others Coles unpub.*

the middle). The great abundance of logboats in the lakes and lochs of Britain and Ireland, and along both major and minor rivers too, shows the importance of this type of boat to early communities, from Mesolithic to medieval (McGrail 1978), and there are plenty of examples from continental north and western Europe (Ellmers 1973; Joncheray 1986; Rieck and Crumlin-Pedersen 1988). The complexity of what is normally considered to be only a hollowed-out log, in such features as expansion, stabilisers, and extension (McGrail 1998), suggests that logboats were the logical precursor of plank-built boats, although such features as these are not at present known from prehistoric north-west Europe. Nonetheless, to work a 15 metre length of fine oak trunk, 90% of which had to be removed by axe, adze and fire, was no mean undertaking.

3. The plank-built boats, as demonstrated by Ferriby and Dover, were impressive artifacts perhaps capable of creating and retaining prestige as well as useful lives as carriers. "The tools of the Iron Age were a prerequisite for the construction of a plank-built boat, which is indeed more seaworthy than a hide boat but more complicated to build" (Marstrander 1963). This disparaging view of Bronze Age tools has been widely disputed (e.g. Christensen 1972; Westerdahl 1985), and Ferriby and Dover prove that Bronze Age tools and technology were perfectly capable of creating complex shapes. In fact, what we now know about Neolithic timber-work shows that the stone axe, wooden wedge and mallet could produce thin and tailored planks, holes, pegs and pins (e.g. Coles, B. and J. 1986); the Swiss lakes had already yielded plenty of this sort of evidence by 1900, and the 7000-year-old Kückhoven well clinches the argument (Weiner 1992). To the small family of extant boats can be added the Hjortspring boat of *c*. 300 BC (Rosenberg 1937) propelled and steered by paddle. Some of the rock carvings show such a craft very clearly (fig.5.3a, small boat in centre), with evenly-curved keel and gunwale lines at fore and aft joined by vertical boards leaving an openwork space, sometimes decorated with shield-like designs. The Hjortspring boat was considered to be a planked version of a hide boat by Marstrander, a view still in some favour.

4. In the farther north of Scandinavia, where timber was perhaps not so abundant or appropriate, and where a light craft for open water was needed for an economy directed in part towards marine resources, hide boats were important and logically were represented in the carvings. "It is doubtful whether (skin boats) have been part of the mainstream of Scandinavian boat-building at any time since the Stone Age" (Hale 1980). That asssertion neatly avoids definition of 'mainstream' and 'Stone Age'. Even so, the northern carvings, and Eurasion boat traditions, combine to suggest that hide boats were an important element in the economies of the north, perhaps into

periods well after the Stone Age. The same might be said about bark boats, a craft never advanced as inspiration for the carvings (fig.5.1b top right might be such a boat).

The problems faced in identifying hide boats in the prehistoric period are formidable, as preservation of the evidence is unlikely to be abundant - if it exists at all. The shale bowl from Caergwrle, Wales, and the gold models from Nors, Denmark, may represent hide boats (Denford and Farrell 1980; Johnstone 1980), but such evidence is in reality pathetic. Classical authors recorded hide boats, probably with sails, plying the Channel waters between Britain and France, and the type must surely have a very long ancestry in north-western Europe. Its presence in the rock carvings can hardly be doubted (fig.5.1a, 5.2j are two possible examples). Hide boats ride high on the surface of the water and in the Baltic or vast inland waters of South Scandinavia they would have been blown merrily along by any following wind - who needs a sail? (Johnstone 1980, 117); so long as you need not turn about.

5. Some carvings probably depict ice-boats rather than water-boats. This can best be seen in the asymmetry of some 'boat' carvings with vertical stem at one end and gently sloped prow at the other (fig.5.2i, 5.2d). The historic representations of northern sledges and, indeed, the vehicles in use at present in some arctic lands, bear a reasonable resemblance to a particular class of rock carving 'boat'. The movement of people, animals and goods over ice and snow is well-attested, and winter carriage is often considered to be far easier than other seasonal travel, avoiding the zigzag lake and stream routes, transfers from pack animal or waggon to boat, uneven ground, dense vegetation, deep and swift and rocky waters. Wooden skis and sledge parts of the early prehistoric period are known from the north, and representations of the sledge are likely to be among the rock carvings. The skiers of Onega are well-known (Hallström 1960, 337). As an aside, there is another kind of sledge, a land sledge, probably in existence in the north from early times; these too seem to be represented in the rock carvings. And just as a waggon could be disassembled for carriage to another place (Piggott 1983, for folding of vehicles), so sewn sledges or boats could be taken apart for ease of transport.

All of this suggests that in the art, everything is possible - nothing much is proved. I think it likely, however, that all of these major types of vehicle, for water and ice, appear in the rock carvings.

The same rather conciliatory and vague conclusions can be drawn about the other debate - the interpretation of purpose. For some authorities, the boat carvings are deeply religious expressions, of fertility wishes and death commemorations. The 'sun-discs' suspended over some boats (fig.5.1c, 5.2b, pl.5.4), the malevolent males standing at stem and stern on some huge boat carvings (pl.5.3), the meekly insignificant crews (fig.5.3f), the occasional adorant humans (fig.5.2l) and the lur-wielding (and blowing?) groups (fig.5.3f) all speak of ceremony, ritual, symbolic expression of a belief system that is mostly beyond our comprehension; in any event, this is no place for such ramblings, as the subject gives rise to lengthy disputations ever since the pioneering days of O. Almgren (fertility, 1926-27), Ekholm (death, 1916), Bing (gods, 1913), Ellmers (carriage of dead, 1973), Müller-Wille (boat of dead, 1974), O. Almgren (invisible god, 1962); this brevity is to deny these authorities their rightful and qualified statements and it totally ignores others, but we should not escape so easily as Malmer who says (1981) that "the ship ... could symbolise almost anything".

I would only suggest here that whatever the impetus, and probably there were many forces at work, there is a strong system in the carvings, perhaps because they could be used as expressions of prestige and importance, in asserting power and cohesion; Østmo (1990) initiates the debate.

It seems clear, to me at least, that the landscape positioning of the boat carvings, many of them near or at the Bronze Age coastline of sea or fjord, or junction of marine waters and freshwater, is very much an outward-looking approach. These were not people content to be tucked away in their little valleys.

*Conclusion*

These boats, so carefully depicted on the rocks of southern Scandinavia, represent a variety of Bronze Age craft. The carvings continue and perpetuate the traditions of the raft, logboat and hide-boat, forms invented long before the first of the carvings were made in southern Scandinavia. But they also indicate the presence of plank-built boats of the Bronze and Iron Ages, and perhaps also of other types of craft not so well surviving in the archaeological record. The later, Viking Age, plank-built boats were capable of open sea travel and it is likely that Bronze Age boats were equally useful, if more restricted in their potential range. It is possible that earlier Bronze Age boats were essentially logboats with additions, later to become more refined and technically advanced by more careful construction of the bottom planking.

By the latest Bronze Age and early Iron Age it is likely that some boats were made for bulk transport and others for long-distance voyages unencumbered by heavy cargo. Such fine vessels, paddled by experienced crews, could have made long journeys in open waters - across the North Sea perhaps (e.g. Butler 1963; O'Connor 1980), over the Channel (e.g. Muckelroy 1981; Cunliffe 1991), through the Baltic (e.g. Mäss 1991; Gimbutas 1965), and along the Atlantic seaboard (e.g. Chevillot and Coffyn 1991). The evidence of existing Bronze Age boats is of boats without sails, and it does seem likely that in this respect, the Scandinavian carved boats are comparable to the Ferriby-Dover boats - inland and sheltered water craft. Nonetheless, I think that the record on the rocks suggests

even more advances, and more potential, in boats that foreshadowed the fine vessels of the later Iron Age in the north. The British boat finds show an impressive mastery of material, and the Scandinavian rock carvings demonstrate an urgency of desire to create expressions of the artifact that ultimately gave humans their unique ability to spread across the world. How else did that Nordic Bronze Age axe come to rest in a native settlement in Upper Canada (Rausing 1977) ? If genuine, and transported soon after manufacture ... now there is a problem for Ted.

*Acknowledgements.* I thank Øle Crumlin-Pedersen and Sean McGrail for advice, and Bryony Coles for comments on the text. I also thank the British Academy for financial support.

## References

Almgren, B. 1962. Den osynliga gudomen. *Proxima Thule*. Stockholm

Almgren, O. 1926-27. *Hällristningar och Kultbruk*. Kungl. Vitterhets Hist. och Antikvitets Akad. Hand. 35.

Bing, J. 1913. Helleristningerstudien. *Oldtiden* III.

Burenhult, G. 1971-72. Rock carving chronology and rock carving ships with sails. *Meddel. fran Lunds Univ. Hist. Mus.* 1971-72, 151-162.

Burenhult, G. 1980. *Götalands Hällristningar*.

Butler, J. 1963. Bronze Age connections across the North Sea. *Palaeohistoria* 9.

Chevillot, C. and Coffyn, A. 1991. *L'âge du bronze atlantique: ses facies, de l'Ecosse à l'Andalousie et leurs relations avec le bronze continental et la mediterranée.*

Christensen, A.E. 1972. Scandinavian ships from earliest times to the Vikings. In G. Bass (ed) *The History of Seafaring*. London.

Christensen, A.E. 1988. Local boats types on the Norwegian coast: a cultural 'Horn of Plenty'. In O.L. Filgueiras (ed) *Local Boats*, 331-349. BAR S438.

Coles, B. and J. 1986. *Sweet Track to Glastonbury*. London.

Cunliffe, B. 1991. Maritime traffic between the continent and Britain. In S. Moscati, O.H. Frey, V. Kruta, B. Raftery and M. Szabo (eds) *The Celts*, 573-580. New York.

Denford, G.T. and Farrell, A.W. 1980. Caergwrle bowl. *Inter. J. Naut. Archaeol.* 9, 183-192.

Ekholm, G. 1916. De skandinaviska hällristningarna och deras betydelse. *Ymer* 1916, 275-308.

Ellmers, D. 1973. Kultbarken, fahren, fischerboote, vorgeschichtliche einbäume in Niedersachsen. *Die Kunde* 24, 23-62.

Fett, E. and P. 1941. *Sydvestnorske Helleristninger. Rogaland og Liste*. Stavanger

Fredskö, Å. 1981. *Hällristningar. Kville härad i Bohuslän. Kville socken*. Göteborg.

Gimbutas, M. 1965. *Bronze Age cultures in central and eastern Europe*. The Hague.

Glob, P.V. 1969. *Helleristninger i Danmark*. Jysk Arkaeol. Selskabs Skrifter VII.

Hagen, A. 1990. *Helleristninger i Noreg*. Oslo.

Hale, J.R. 1980. Plank-built in the Bronze Age. *Antiquity* 54, 118-127.

Hallström, G. 1960. *Monumental art of northern Sweden from the Stone Age. Nämforsen and other localities*. Stockholm.

Johnstone, P. 1972. Bronze Age sea trial. *Antiquity* 46, 269-274.

Johnstone, P. 1980. *The Sea-craft of Prehistory*. London.

Joncheray, D. 1986. *Les embarcations monoxyles dans la region pays de la Loire*. Etudes prehist. et hist. des pays de la Loire 9.

Malmer, M.P. 1981. *A chorological study of North European rock art*. Kungl. Vitterhets Hist. och Antikvitets Akad. Antikvar. 32.

Marstrander, S. 1963. *Østfolds Jordbruksristninger, Skebjerg*. Inst. for Sammenlignende Kulturforskning.

Mäss, V. 1991. Prospects for underwater archaeology in the eastern Baltic. *Int. J. Naut. Archaeol.* 20, 313-320.

McGrail, S. 1978. *Logboats of England and Wales. BAR* 51.

McGrail, S. 1981. *The Brigg 'raft' and her prehistoric environment. BAR* 89.

McGrail, S. 1990. Boats and boatmanship in the late prehistoric southern North Sea and Channel region. In S.McGrail (ed) *Maritime Celts, Frisians and Saxons*, 32-48. CBA Res. Rep. 71.

McGrail, S. 1991. Early sea voyages. *Int. J. Naut. Archaeol.* 20, 85-93.

McGrail, S. and Kentley, E. (eds) 1985. *Sewn Plank Boats. BAR* S276.

Muckelroy, K. 1981. Middle Bronze Age trade between Britain and Europe: a maritime perspective. *Proc. Prehist. Soc.* 47, 275-297.

Müller-Wille, M. 1968-69. Bestattung im Boot. Studien zu einer nordeuropäischen Grabsitte. *Offa*, 25-26.

O'Connor, B. 1980. *Cross-Channel relations in the later Bronze Age. BAR* S91.

Piggott, S. 1983. *The earliest wheeled transport. From the Atlantic coast to the Caspian Sea*. London.

Rausing, G. 1977. Bronzealderens Columbus. *Skalk* 1977, 1, 9-10.

Rieck, F. and Crumlin-Pedersen, O. 1988. *Bäde fra Danmarks Oldtid*. Roskilde.

Rosenberg, G. 1937. *Hjortspringfundet*. Nord. Oldtidsminder III i.

Sognnes, K. 1987. Bergkunsten i Stjødal 2. Typologi og Kronologi i nedre Stjørdal. *Gunneria* 56. Trondheim.

Weiner, J. 1992. Eine bandkeramische Siedlung mit Brunnen bei Erkelenz-Kückhoven. *Schriften des Heimatvereins der Erkelenzer Lande* 12, 17-33.

Westerdahl, C. 1985. Sewn boats of Sweden. In S. McGrail and E. Kentley (eds) *Sewn Plank Boats. BAR* S276.

Wright, E.V. 1990. *The Ferriby Boats. Sea craft of the Bronze Age*. London.

Østmo, E. 1990. *Helleristninger av sørskandinaviske former på det indre østlandet*. Univ. Oldsak. Skrifter 12.

Østmo, E. 1992. Helleristninger i et utkantstrøk. Bidrag til skipshistorien fra nye jernalderrisninger på Dalbo i Baerum. *Varia* 24.

# 6

# PREHISTORIC HOKO RIVER CORDAGE
## A new line on northwest coast prehistory

### *Dale Croes*

Archaeological sites with preserved cordage from around the world reveal distinctive information about site use. Ted Wright, who has pioneered much work on the manufacture and use of the basic one-strand cordage category called "withies" (called withe in our area of the world!), has shown how these withies are used in sewing boats and other prehistoric objects. Using his information we have gained much insight as to how prehistoric peoples of the Northwest Coast of North America manufactured and used cedar limb withies to sew together watertight cooking and storage bentwood boxes, sew the prow and stern pieces and seat struts into their canoes, and literally tie up their house walls boards and poles on the huge shed-roof longhouses characteristic of Pacific Northwest coastal villages (Croes 1980a). Besides withies, Northwest Coast sites produce numerous examples of multiple-strand twisted and braided lines functionally used as general purpose lines, clothing warps, nets, fishline leaders, harpoon lines and wedge collars. These general cordage types and functional categories will be discussed with reference to the early Hoko River Archaeological Site on the Northwest tip of Washington State, U.S.A.

Since the late 1960s sizeable collections of cordage artifacts have been recovered from Northwest Coast wet (waterlogged) sites, with two, Hoko River and Ozette Village, recording over 2,000 examples (fig. 6.1). Recorded time-depth for cordage collections now reaches 4,500 years ago with the recent recovery of a small sample from the Glenrose and St. Mungo Cannery wet components on the Fraser River Delta, British Columbia (Eldridge 1991).

Usually other wet site perishable artifacts, such as carved wooden art and complex basketry, gain much of the public and analytical attention (Daugherty and Friedman 1983, Bernick 1988, Croes 1976, 1980b, 1988, 1992a, 1992b). However prehistoric cordage collections do pro-vide sensitive stylistic characteristics that can be used to further evaluate the degrees of similarity observed on basketry, lithic, bone and shell artifacts from Northwest Coast wet and shell midden sites (Croes 1989a).

Using the Hoko River wet site as a focus, a site that has recorded more cordage to date than any other Northwest Coast wet site (n = 2,323 examples), I will characterize the cordage research results.

The Hoko River Archaeological Site Complex provides evidence for 3,000 years of coastal occupation. It contains two temporally distinct major site areas: (1) an upriver waterlogged (wet) site and adjoining (dry) campsite area (45CA213), dating 3000—2000 BP; and (2) a river mouth shell midden living area within a large rockshelter (45CA21), occupied from *ca.* 1000—100 BP.

Archaeological data recovery from both site areas provided distinct kinds of prehistoric remains. The Hoko River wet site provides excellent preservation of perishable artifacts, allowing a much more complete understanding of procurement and processing equipment, such as fishing gear, butchering tools, and transporting equipment (i.e., pack baskets), as well as sensitive styles of basketry and cordage for intrasite comparisons and good preservation of faunal and floral remains reflecting resource uses (see Croes & Blinman 1980, Croes 1992a, 1992b).

Geomorphologically, the Hoko River wet site contains at least 45 separate and sequentially deposited vegetal mat layers deposited along a river point bar shore next to a major fishing camp (Stucki 1983). The contiguous layer sequence represents the time period from 2,600 to 3,000 years BP. The river bottom waterlogged site deposits have been tectonically uplifted a mm/year since originally formed, now being an average 3 m higher and available for

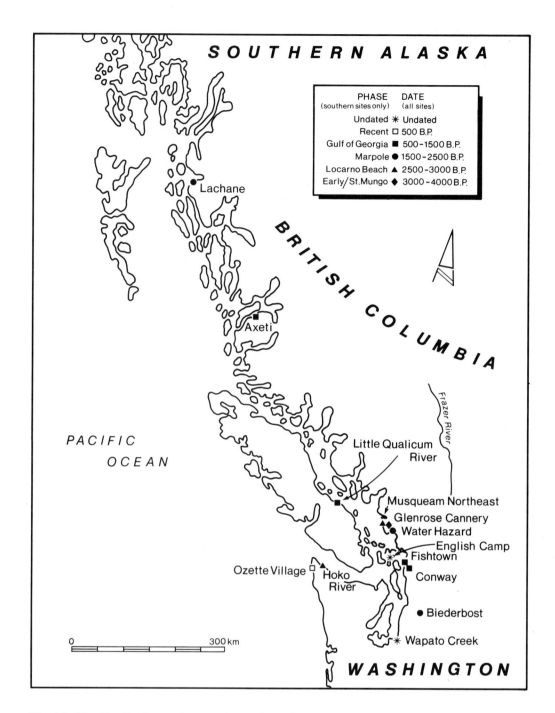

*Fig. 6.1 The distribution and approximate date of investigated wet sites on the Northwest Coast of North America.*

excavation during mean to low tides (Croes and Blinman 1980, Stucki 1983). Since these deposits are being rapidly eroded by a change in the river course, we have spent 9 summer field seasons (1977 through 1987) recovering an estimated 10% of the wet site deposits. The layers with 100 or more artifacts recovered (8 main layers) demonstrated consistent mean and standard deviation percentage of the main artifact categories recovered from each layer; therefore we can predict the percentage expected of cordage, basketry, wood working tools, fishing hooks, and other categories, from any given layer. Since this is a multi-layer wet site, we carefully compared artifacts from all layers to see if styles or types of perishable artifacts

changed over the 400 year time period, but found remarkable continuity throughout (see Croes 1992a).

At the nearby wet site of Ozette Village, comparable numbers of recorded cordage artifacts were recovered from a late village site (n = 2,014 reported examples; Croes 1980a). This site represents three complete houses and three partial houses recovered from under a mudslide (Samuels 1983, 1991). Over 40,000 house structural remains, with many of the house planks, poles, and posts broken into many pieces by the mudslide, were recovered from a section of a major village dating to approximately 250 years ago by tree-ring analysis (Draper 1989, Gleeson

1983, Mauger 1978, 1991). Therefore, as a unique Northwest Coast wet site setting, Ozette represents a point in time, all preserved wood and fiber artifacts coming from a large community (Croes 1992a).

At Hoko River cordage represents 61% of all artifacts recovered, far above the 12% indicated for the Ozette Village collection, but similar to some other wet sites (e.g., 63% for Little Qualicum River (Bernick 1983) and 56% for Axeti (Hobler 1970)). This discrepancy is no doubt due to site deposition, with (1) Ozette Village containing everything in a section of a village that was encased, pompeii-style, under a mudslide and (2) all other Northwest Coast wet sites, to date, representing discard deposits next to villages or fishing camps where broken items had been thrown in a wet setting and became preserved through waterlogging (Croes 1992a). Therefore in the Ozette site one expects a wide diversity of domestic and structural remains, whereas at other wet sites one would expect concentrations of discarded broken objects. As expected, broken cordage and associated artifacts are common in these wet middens.

## Hoko River and Northwest Coast Cordage Comparative Analysis

In this Northwest Coast study, cordage is defined as: *any line, commonly categorized as a rope, cord or string, that is twisted, braided or a plain thin strip of bark, limb, twig or root* (Croes 1980a, 4). This definition includes the general categories of rope, cord, and string, and the cordage forms of lines, loops, nets, and wedge collars.

The Hoko River cordage are made of a number of different materials, techniques, numbers of strands, and

| Definition | | | Frequency | |
|---|---|---|---|---|
| **HO-C1** | | | | |
| *Material:* | cedar bough | | n=600 | 26% |
| *Construction tech:* | twist | | | |
| *No. of strands:* | 1 | | | |
| *Lay/twist:* | -/L | | | |
| *Gauge sizes (diameters):* | | | | |
| | a. string: | n=519 | 22% | |
| | b. cord: | n=81 | 3% | |
| **HO-C9** | | | | |
| *Material:* | spruce root | | n=1481 | 63% |
| Construction tech: | twist | | | |
| No. of strands: | 2 | | | |
| Lay/twist: | Z/R | | | |
| Gauge sizes (diameters): | | | | |
| | a. string: | n=1369 | 59% | |
| | b. cord: | n=111 | 5% | |
| | c. rope: | n=1 | - | |

*Fig. 6.2 Examples of Hoko River cordage class-type (HO-C#) definitions, with the two most common cordage types defined (Croes 1980a, 1980c, 1989a).*

gauges. These cordage attributes (or modes) and their combinations into cordage classes (or types) are considered in this paper and compared with similar cordage modes and types from other Northwest Coast wet sites. The functional context of the cordage is discussed, placing these artifacts into the overall site-use setting.

The modes of Hoko River cordage—the construction materials, the construction techniques (including number of strands and lay/twist), and the gauge size—can be combined to form a paradigmatic classification of Hoko River cordage types. This is considered a stylistic/technological classification, and its main purpose is to illustrate the range of cordage types and also to create explicit class units for comparison with the same class units found at other Northwest Coast wet sites (fig. 6.2).

Overall 16 cordage types and 36 subtypes (diameter gauge classes) of cordage occur. The frequencies of different types vary greatly, with spruce root two-strand lines (HO-C9) being the most common (n = 1,473 examples, 63%) followed by cedar bough one-strand withies (HO-C1, n = 607 examples, 26%). The remaining 11% include a variety of different kinds of twisted bough and root cordage and examples of braided cedar bark and strap (typically binding) cordage types.

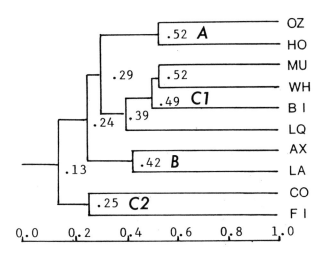

*Fig. 6.3 Dendrogram representing average linkage cluster analysis of Northwest Coast wet site cordage types on a matrix of Jaccard's coefficients. Degree of similarity: 1 = complete similarity; 0 = no similarity.*

These classes and subclasses of cordage have been compared with similar ones occurring at the ten most investigated Northwest Coast wet sites (fig. 6.1, Croes 1980a, 1989a), and now with the addition of new wet site data from Hoko River, Little Qualicum River and a 2,000 year old wet site recently examined on the Fraser River, Water Hazard (Bernick 1989). Sixty six cordage subclasses are compared using an average-linkage cluster analysis on a matrix of Jaccard coefficient (fig. 6.3; definitions of all classes are in Croes 1980a). The resulting updated dendrogram shows a closer relationship between Hoko River and Ozette Village, a linking of Water Hazard with 2-3,000 year old wet sites in the Gulf of Georgia/Puget Sound, and an offshoot clustering of the Puget Sound sites of Conway and Fishtown, which, unfortunately, have too small a cordage sample size for serious consideration (n = 12 and 9 examples respectively, whereas all other site cordage collections have 50 or more examples compared).

In general, this resulting dendrogram compares well with the regional clustering of sites as shown in the basketry analyses, which are probably more complex and therefore sensitive artifacts (Bernick 1988, Croes 1989a, 1992a, 1992b). The addition of the 2,000 year old materials from Water Hazard nicely links with the Gulf of Georgia/Puget Sound region and early cordage from Biederbost and Musqueam Northeast. Since these data continue to be consistent with a model of regional style continuity, these patterns of basketry and cordage do not appear to be coincidental, but likely the result of continuity of traditions in at least the West Coast and Gulf of Georgia/Puget Sound regions of the Northwest Coast for at least 3,000 years.

## Hoko River Cordage and other Northwest Coast Cordage Functional Analysis

Forms of Hoko River cordage include lines, wedge collars, fishline leaders, nets, rigid lattice works, cedar bough storage bundles, small diameter circulates, large diameter circulates, twig bundles, cherry/spruce-root binding elements and spliced-in looped ends (Table 1). In this paper the common form of cordage lines and wedge collars, as well as nets, will be discussed.

| Form | | Number | % |
|---|---|---|---|
| 1. | Lines | 2,247 | 98 |
| 2. | Collars (for wooden wedges) | 25 | 1 |
| 3. | Nets | 6 | |
| 4. | Rigid Lattice-work | 2 | |
| 5. | Small Diameter Circulates | 1 | |
| 6. | Large Diameter Circulates | 2 | |
| 7. | Twig Bundles | 1 | |
| 8. | Cedar Bough Storage Bundles | 3 | |
| 9. | Cherry Bark/Split Root Binding Elements | 33 | 1 |
| 10. | Spliced-in Looped End | 3 | |

*TABLE 1* Hoko River Cordage Forms

## Lines

Independent lines are by far the most frequent example and typically occur as small broken pieces. Two cordage types make up 89% of all lines, the two-strand rootlet strings (HO-C9, 63%) and the one-strand twisted withies (HO-C1, 26%) (fig. 6.2).

The two-strand rootlet string lines have been functionally associated as (1) the sewing element of the frequent sewn tule mats (HO-M1, n = 26 examples), (2) the twining

selvage element for the shredded cedar bark capes/skirts (HO-F1, n = 15 examples), and (3) the looped fishline leaders, tied with a square knot and found attached with a clove hitch to the knob ends of the frequent composite and bentwood hooks (Croes and Blinman 1980, Hoff 1980, Pl. 1a-1c).

Their high frequency at the site is believed to associate most with the fragmenting of sewn tule mats thought to be used to cover the temporary fishing camp shelters. An average 4 x 6 foot mat, constructed in the manner common to the site, would require from 75 to 90 feet of string sewing element. Each shelter might require 6-10 mats to cover the walls, meaning up to 900 feet of string represented in all the mats on one dwelling (remains of a Hoko River camp shelter area excavated in the dry site is described in Howes 1982). These mats would eventually wear out, and possibly some of the old sewing elements could be reused in making new mats, but also much might be simply discarded with worn out pieces of matting. Since the tule materials is very fragile, the 2-strand rootlet strings would best survive and be found as smaller pieces.

The twined edging of shredded bark capes/skirts would preserve best, often with only a small remnant of the shredded bark still attached (pl.6.5). These broken cape/skirt string selvage fragments would add to the number of spruce rootlet strings found at the site.

While cordage contribute 61% of the Hoko River perishable artifacts, fishhooks (pl.6.1-2) are the second most frequent artifact (n = 463 examples, 12% of the artifacts). Two fishhook forms are found, one a bentwood (30%) and another a V-shaped composite (60%), with the remaining 10% being preforms to construct bentwood hooks. Both forms have a knob used to secure the two-strand string leaders. Fishline leaders as broken would also be discarded if too small to reuse, providing another source for the frequent number of strings found.

The use of two-strand spruce rootlet strings in constructing the above three common Hoko River artifact categories—sewn tule mats, selvage of shredded bark cape/skirts, and fishline leaders/lines—would best explain the very high frequency of this type of cordage at this site.

The one-strand twisted cedar bough withies (HO-C1) represent over one quarter of the cordage recovered, but have not been found with direct functional associations at the site. However their use can also be predicted from the expected construction of pole framed dwellings and drying racks. As at Ozette Village, the majority of these withies probably were used in the construction of the dwellings, but instead of holding wall boards between double rows of poles as seen at Ozette (Croes 1980a, Mauger 1978, 1991), they would be used to tie together the pole framework of the dwellings that would then be covered with tule mats and bark shingles. Withies would also be used to tie together the pole framework of the drying rakes. In experimental reconstructions of both dwellings and drying rakes, we found cedar bough withies

Dale Croes

work very well in holding the poles to one another. Such a high frequency of withies would correspond to their importance in constructing these pole structures at this temporary fishing camp.

Most of the remaining 11% of the cordage lines are a variety of two- and three-strand cedar bough, cedar bark and/or spruce root strings, cords and ropes), three strand cedar bark braids, and cedar bark, cherry bark and splint bough/root strap cordage. They are in low numbers and any direct functional associations are not always obvious, though they certainly may have had multiple tying and binding uses in the fishing camp context.

*Wedge Collars*

The cordage wedge collars typically are two- or three-strand twisted cedar bough grommet forms that are found both independently and on the poll ends of wooden wedges (pl. 6.3-4). These collars always are a single loop, never seen with a double ring as found at Ozette Village and Water Hazard (Croes 1980a, Bernick 1989). The number of strands creating these loops varied from two to four, probably most dependent on the length of the original cedar bough withie forming the tight loop. The independent collars averaged a mean 4.3 cm in outer diameter (n = 16 examples, SD = 0.9 cm), approximately in the range of the average diameter for collars recorded at Ozette Village (4.5 cm diameter, Croes 1980a, 112). These collars would have prevented the wooden wedge from splitting while it was pounded into a log in the process of getting firewood or splitting boards. This general form of collar is found at most Northwest Coast wet sites, and normally of 3-strand, Z-twist construction (Bernick 1989, Croes 1980a, 1980b, 1980c, 1989b, Inglis 1976). Anthropologist Franz Boas provided a valuable ethnographic account of the manufacture and application of wedge collars by the Kwakiutl, which may apply for the past 3,000 years along the Northwest Coast:

> Crowns for wedges and chisels are made of cedar-withies in the following manner: a long withie is turned into a ring about 5 cm. in diameter, beginning at the middle of the withe. First the thick end is twisted in and out through the ring until one circuit has been completed. Then the thin end is treated in the same way, so that a complete ring, consisting of a three-strand rope, is made. This ring is placed on the slightly sharpened butt-end of the wedge, which is battered down until it is quite flat and the ring is held firmly in place (1909, 380).

*Nets*

One large fragment of net was recovered from the Hoko River, along with up to 5 very small fragments of isolated knot segments. The larger piece (215/AS/1) appears to be constructed of split spruce-bough or twig material (approximately .4 to .5 cm wide splint strips).

The net is formed with square knots, and there is

approximately 5 cm between knots. A relatively wide-gauge net, this example with an attached anchor stone probably was used in fishing activities at the site, and possibly as a gill net (Croes 1980a).

Hoko River is the only Northwest Coast wet site so far recorded with nets made from one-strand splint limb elements. At Ozette Village, Musqueam Northeast and Water Hazard the nets are made of 2-strand cordage, using spruce root elements at Ozette Village and cedar bark at Musqueam Northeast and Water Hazard (Croes 1980a, Bernick 1989, Stevenson 1989). The two-strand cordage net has a Z-lay at Ozette and Musqueam Northeast, but a S-lay at Water Hazard (Stevenson 1989). All sites use square-knots as the netting knot, and this typically is the net knot tied by hand, without a netting needle (Ashley 1944, 64-65).

*Summary and Conclusions*

Hoko River cordage is characterized by a focus on 2-strand rootlet strings and 1-strand withies, both of which probably owe their abundance to their use in the construction of shelter mat covers and frames, and drying rake frames at this temporary fishing camp location. Beyond this focus, the overall occurrence of different varieties of Hoko River cordage modes, classes (types) and functional forms reflects a basic cordage technology which shares the greatest degree of similarity with those from Ozette Village. This stylistic/technological relationship corresponds with the general basketry style similarities between these two sites and lends additional support to the hypothesis of cultural continuity in this West Coast region of the Northwest Coast for approximately 3,000 years (Croes 1977, 1989a, 1992a, 1992b, Croes and Blinman 1980).

The functional forms of Hoko River cordage associates with mat forms (sewn tule mats), fishing activities (fishline leaders), clothing (twined shredded cedar bark capes/skirts), woodworking practices (wooden wedge collars), procurement techniques (nets and open lattice-work), and manufacturing activities (cherry bark/spruce root binding elements).

The abundant use of two-strand spruce rootlet strings is unique to this Northwest Coast wet site, and demonstrates an emphasis on a high quality, strong string element for many tasks. Replication experiments suggest that these strings could be made at about two meters an hour once roots are stripped, soaked in water and ready to use. Tensile strength tests using replicated rootlet strings indicate that single elements usually could hold from 30 to 50 lbs pull before breaking and double strands (such as for fishhook leaders) held 70 lbs (Jones-Brooks 1980). These tests indicate that sewn tule mats were built for considerable strength and probably durability at Hoko, especially since ethnographic examples are typically sewn with twisted tule strings, which must be relatively weaker. And their use as fishline leaders should have been very effective for taking, for example, 25 lbs halibut, as characteristic of the prehistoric and abundant halibut remains

36

and the Hoko fishing banks today (D. Huelsbeck, *pers. comm.* 1992).

Therefore Hoko River cordage associates with many of the activities participated in by the people who occupied this 3,000 year old fishing camp. It also has proven to be stylistically and technologically useful for regional comparative studies, complementing basketry studies that produce regional continuity patterns for at least 3,000 years on the Northwest Coast of North America.

*Acknowledgements.* I would like to particularly thank Ted Wright for his earlier encouragement, sharing of personal research, and friendship. The many articles he sent to me have been building blocks for research when considering Northwest Coast cordage. I would also like to thank the editors for making this volume possible. In particular, John Coles has supported wet sites research on the Northwest Coast of North America and made it possible that this effort be included in international works such as this volume. In terms of this paper, the Hoko River Project research is co-sponsored by the Makah Tribal Nation, and has been made possible through support of the M.J. Murdock Charitable Trust, the National Endowment for the Humanities, and Ray and Jean Auel. Numerous project researchers, Makah community members, field personnel and students have contributed to data recovery, analysis and reporting. Though this research owes its existence to these and many previous and current researchers, the summary and conclusions remain the responsibility of the author.

# References

Ashley, C.W. 1944. *The Ashley Book of Knots*. Garden City, New York: Doubleday and Company, Inc.

Bernick, K. 1983. *A Site Catchment Analysis of the Little Qualicum River Site, DiSc 1: a wet site on the east coast of Vancouver Island, B.C.* Ottawa: National Museum of Man Mercury Series, 118.

Bernick, K. 1988. The Potential of Basketry for Reconstructing Cultural Diversity on the Northwest Coast. In R. Auger, M.F. Glass, S. MacEachern and P. McCartney (eds), *Ethnicity and Culture*, 251-257. University of Calgary, Calgary: Proceedings of the 18th Annual Chacmool Conference, Archaeological Association.

Bernick, K. 1989. *Water Hazard (DgRs 30) Artifact Recovery Project Report, Permit 1988-55.* Victoria: Archaeology and Outdoor Recreation Branch, Ministry of Municipal Affairs, Recreation and Culture, Province of British Columbia.

Boas, F. 1909. *The Kwakiutl of Vancouver Island.* Washington, DC: American Museum of Natural History, Memoir 8.

Croes, D.R. (ed) 1976. *The Excavation of Water-saturated Archaeological Sites (Wet Sites) on the Northwest Coast of North America.* Ottawa: National Museum of Man Mercury Series, 50.

Croes, D.R. 1977. *Basketry from the Ozette Village Archaeological Site: A Technological, Functional and Comparative Study.* Ann Arbor: University Microfilms 77-25, 762, Ann Arbor.

Croes, D.R. 1980a. *Cordage from the Ozette Village Archaeological Site: A Technological, Functional and Comparative Study.* Washington State University, Pullman: Laboratory of Archaeology and History, 9.

Croes, D.R. 1980b. Basketry Artifacts. In D.R. Croes and E. Blinman (ed), *Hoko River: A 2,500 Year Old Fishing Camp on the Northwest Coast of North America.* Washington State University, Pullman: Laboratory of Anthropology Reports of Investigations 58, 188-222.

Croes, D.R. 1980c. Wooden wedges. In D.R. Croes and E. Blinman (ed), *Hoko River: A 2,500 Year Old Fishing Camp on the Northwest Coast of North America.* Washington State University, Pullman: Laboratory of Anthropology Reports of Investigations 58, 268-273.

Croes, D.R. 1988. The Significance of the 3,000 BP Hoko River Waterlogged Fishing Camp in our Overall Understanding of Southern Northwest Coast Cultural Evolution. In B. Purdy (ed), *Wet Site Archaeology.* New Jersey: Telford Press.

Croes, D.R. 1989a. Prehistoric Ethnicity on the Northwest Coast of North America, An Evaluation of Style in Basketry and Lithics. *Research in Anthropological Archaeology*, R. Whallon, (ed), New York: Academic Press.

Croes, D.R. 1989b. Lachane Basketry and Cordage: A Technological, Functional and Comparative Study. *Canadian Journal of Archaeology*, 13, 165-205.

Croes, D.R. 1992a. An Evolving Revolution in Wet Site Research on the Northwest Coast of North America. In Bryony Coles (ed). *The Wetland Revolution in Prehistory*, 99-111. Exeter, England: WARP Occasional Paper 6.

Croes, D.R. 1992b. Exploring Prehistoric Subsistence Change on the Northwest Coast. In D.R. Croes, R.A. Hawkins and B.L. Isaac (eds), *Long-Term Subsistence Change in Prehistoric North America*, Research in Economic Anthropology, Special Supplement 6, 337-366. Greenwich, Connecticut: JAI Press, Inc.

Croes, D.R. and Blinman, E. (eds) 1980. *Hoko River: A 2,500 Year Old Fishing Camp on the Northwest Coast of North America.* Washington State University, Pullman: Laboratory of Anthropology Reports of Investigations 58.

Daugherty R.D. and Friedman, J. 1983. An Introduction to Ozette Art. In R.L. Carlson (ed), *Indian Art Traditions of the Northwest Coast*, 183-195. Simon Fraser University, Burnaby, B.C.: Archaeology Press.

Draper, J.A. 1989. *Ozette Lithic Analysis.* Washington State University, Pullman, Washington 99164.

Eldridge, M. 1991. *The Glenrose Cannery Wet Component: A Significance Assessment.* Permit 1990-24, Victoria: British Columbia Archaeology Branch.

Gleeson, P. (ed) 1983. *Ozette Dendrochronological Studies.* Washington State University, Pullman: Laboratory of Anthropology.

Hobler, P. 1970. Survey and Excavation in the Vicinity of Bella Coola. *B.C. Studies*, 6-7, 77-94.

Howes, D.W. 1982. Spatial Analysis at a Northwest Coast Fishing Camp: The Hoko River Site. In D.R. Croes (ed), *Interim Annual Report, Hoko River Archaeological Project, Phases XIII & XIV*, Attachment N, Washington D.C.: National Endowment for the Humanities.

Inglis, R. 1976. 'Wet' Site Distribution - The Northern Case, GbTo 33 - The Lachane Site. In D.R. Croes (ed), *The Excavation of Water-saturated Archaeological Sites*

*Dale Croes*

*(Wet Sites) on the Northwest Coast of North America.*
Ottawa: National Museum of Man Mercury Series, 50,
158-185.

Jones-Brooks, J.V. 1980. Tensile Strength of Replicated
Hoko River Cordage. In D.R. Croes and E. Blinman
(eds), *Hoko River: A 2,500 Year Old Fishing Camp on
the Northwest Coast of North America.* Washington
State University, Pullman: Laboratory of Anthropology
Reports of Investigations 58, 257-268.

Mauger, J.E. 1978. Shed Roof Houses at the Ozette Archaeological Site: A Protohistoric Architectural System. *Washington Archaeological Research Center* 73, Washington State University, Pullman.

Mauger, J.E. 1991. Shed-Roof Houses at Ozette and in a
Regional Perspective. In S.R. Samuels (ed), *Ozette
Archaeological Project Research Reports, Volume I,
House Structure and Floor Midden* Washington State
University, Pullman: Laboratory of Anthropology Re-
ports of Investigations 63, 28-173.

Samuels, S.R. 1983. *Spatial Analysis of Ozette House Floor
Deposits.* Washington State University, Pullman: Laboratory of Anthropology.

Samuels, S.R. 1991. Patterns in Ozette Floor Middens:
Reflections of Social Units. In S.R. Samuels (ed), *Ozette
Archaeological Project Research Reports, Volume I,
House Structure and Floor Midden* Washington State
University, Pullman: Laboratory of Anthropology Re-
ports of Investigations 63, 176-270.

Stevenson A. 1989. Netting and Associated Cordage. In K.
Bernick (ed), *Water Hazard (DgRs 30) Artifact Recov-
ery Project Report, Permit 1988-55,* Appendix A, Vic-
toria: Archaeology and Outdoor Recreation Branch,
Ministry of Municipal Affairs, Recreation and Culture,
Province of British Columbia.

Stucki, B.R. 1983. Fluvial Processes and the Formation of the
Hoko River Archaeological Site (45CA213), Olympic
Peninsula, Washington. In D.R. Croes (ed), *Interim
annual report, Hoko River Archaeological Project, Phase
XIII & XIV,* Attachment K, Washington D.C.: National
Endowment for the Humanities.

# 7

# THE NYDAM SHIPS
## Old and new investigations at a classic site

### Øle Crumlin-Pedersen and Flemming Rieck

The Nydam Boat or Ship, now on exhibition at Archäologisches Landesmuseum in Schleswig, Northern Germany, is the largest object recovered from the Nydam Bog in South Jutland, Denmark. This bog was a holy lake where, in the 3rd-5th century, the local population deposited offerings of war-booty on several occasions. The ship itself has a key position in the study of the history of shipbuilding in Northern Europe. No other ships have been found that have been able to challenge the position of this vessel as the type of ship that:

- introduced clinker construction with iron fastenings in Scandinavia,
- introduced rowing technology in Scandinavian vessels, and
- brought the Angles and Saxons to Britain.

Yet the Nydam Ship is not a singular find, but one out of several vessels found in the bog. The history of this find is dramatic - and the last chapters of the drama are yet to be written!

The Nydam Ship has been described in detail by its excavator, the Danish archaeologist Conrad Engelhardt (1865, 1866a, 1866b), and by the Norwegian archaeologist Hakon Shetelig (1930). The German naval architect G. Timmermann studied the building process of the ship in 1941, and in 1963 the Swedish ship-archaeologist Harald Åkerlund published a careful analysis of the find. Recently the present authors and others have presented old and new details of the find in various publications (Rieck & Crumlin-Pedersen 1988; Crumlin-Pedersen 1990; Bonde 1990; Bonde et al. 1991). Besides the ship is a standard reference in practically all publications of the archaeology of the

period. Thus one may find reflected in this list of references the international interest in this outstanding find.

In fact the Nydam find became a matter of international concern at a very high level very soon after it was found late in 1863. This was because a war broke out between Denmark and Germany by New year 1864. As this was won by the united Prussian-Austrian troops, taking control of the former Danish duchy Slesvig-Holsten, the Nydam find was specifically mentioned in the peace-treaty in 1865 to be taken over by the Germans. But Conrad Engelhardt (pl.7.1) had fled to Copenhagen with all records of the excavation, including the files of the Flensborg Collection of which he was in charge before the war. The boat had been mounted for exhibition in Flensborg and could not be moved, but all other finds had mysteriously disappeared, and no officials could remember anything about where they were. It took a reward of 25,000 Rigsdaler paid to an anonymous informer by the Ministry of Education in Kiel, before the 32 boxes of the Iron Age war-spoils were located in Denmark and handed over to the Germans (Ilkjær & Lønstrup, 1984).

This incident is a good example of the problems involved for anyone who wants to study the details of Engelhardt's excavations in Nydam in 1863. He was working in a race against time and had to cover some of his moves. The political situation was very tense, and a Prussian occupation was expected at any time. In spite of this the Danish king Frederik 7th, who was actively engaged in archaeology, took a day off from his official functions on October 27th 1863 to watch Engelhardt bringing a proper full size vessel up from the bog. But with the death of the king only two weeks later, the occupation

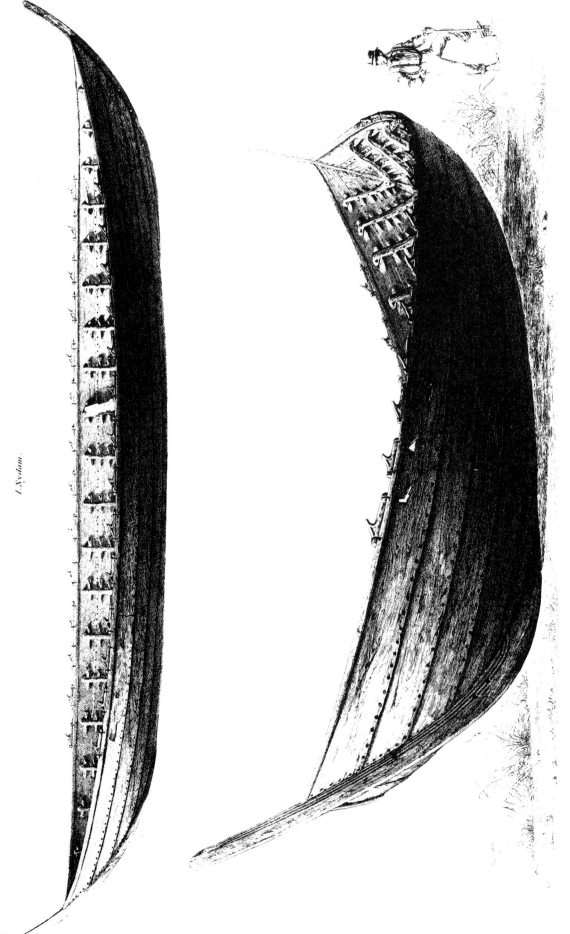

I.Nydam.

40

Fig.7.1 The Nydam Ship found and excavated in 1863. A somewhat romanticized drawing by Magnus Peterson. From Engelhardt 1865.

could be expected at any time. In fact the Prussians invaded Holsten on December 24th 1863 and Slesvig on February 1st 1864. The Danish defence line lay in the immediate vicinity of the Nydam bog and it came to intense fighting in the area before the Danish troops were forced to withdraw.

These conditions were not favourable for archaeology, and it is admirable that Engelhardt was able, nevertheless, to present a monograph on the results of the excavation in 1865 from his new post as archaeologist at the National Museum in Copenhagen (fig.7.1). Over the following years he excavated a number of similar war-spoil finds elsewhere in Denmark, waiting for a chance to return to the Nydam bog to conclude his work here, as he had quite evidently been cut off abruptly from his studies of this site.

In Denmark it was expected after the war that either the whole region lost or at least the Slesvig region, from the Kongeaa river in the North to the Eider river in the South, would be returned to Denmark as a result of the peace-negotiations. However, it was not until 1920 that the northern part of the Slesvig region was reunited with Denmark after the Versailles Treaty. At that time the present borderline was established on the basis of a referendum, - and then Nydam again turned Danish, as it has remained since.

Engelhardt died in 1881, and thus he did not live to resume his excavations in Nydam. But before leaving the area in 1864 he instructed his local foreman Povl Adam not to tell the Germans any details about the location of the finds in the bog. Engelhardt did this, it seems, because he found another boat in the bog which was not excavated but covered over in order to keep it a secret until future excavation could take place under Danish control.

If this statement is correct this vessel would be boat no. 4 located in the bog by Engelhardt. At first he had found parts of a vessel of oak that had been chopped to pieces (fig.7.3) before being deposited in the lake, - just like many of the weapons that had been deliberately damaged and bent prior to their deposition. Then came as the second vessel the splendid oak ship which is now in Schleswig. Shortly before the excavation was interrupted a large boat of pine was found, the one raised under royal supervision. The keel of this boat was recorded in a sketch, but all timbers raised had to be left on the site. Here they were later chopped up to serve as firewood for the troops invading the area (fig.7.2).

These three vessels are reported by Engelhardt in his publication of the Nydam find, whereas the fourth vessel is only to be found in his publications in a table in the volume on another find of war-spoils, from Kragehul (1867), listing three boats and fragments of a fourth as found in Nydam. Even if the text in the Kragehul publication is so clear that a printing error can be ruled out, this may only be taken as an indication of a possible fourth boat in the bog.

There is, however, another source of information on this question. This is a note from H. P. Hanssen who was born 1862 on a farm in the neighbourhood of Nydam (Hanssen 1925). His family was well known after the war for their patriotic support of the Danish cause in the ongoing struggle between Danish and German culture in the region. Around 1880 he went fishing in the Nydam bog and met Povl Adam. They discussed Engelhardt's work and the sad fact that there was no prospect for a continuation of that in the near future. Then Povl Adam disclosed the secret of his life to the young man. He told him that just before the excavation was brought to a halt they had found

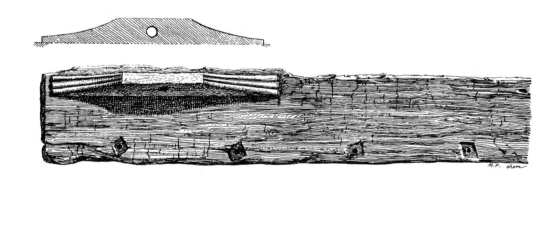

*Fig.7.2 The only parts of the pine boat which survived the war in 1864. The rowlocks and the fragment of a plank are in the collections of the Danish National Museum. From Engelhardt 1865.*

*Fig.7.3 Fragments of planking and gunwale from the chopped up oak boat found by Engelhardt in 1863. From Engelhardt 1865.*

another boat ('the fourth boat') and kept it a secret in order to enable Engelhardt to return to the site when the area, hopefully, was returned to Denmark. Now both Povl Adam and Engelhardt were ageing, and Adam feared that they would both die -and with them this secret knowledge - before Danish archaeologists got a chance to return to the site. He pointed out to young Hanssen the position of the 'fourth boat' in the bog, and by probing with the fishing rod they could feel what they thought were the timbers of the boat deep in the bog.

H. P. Hanssen marked out the position of the suggested boat on the surface of the bog, and soon afterwards he went abroad for studies. When he returned in 1888 both Engelhardt and Povl Adam had died. On inspecting the bog he found that the markers had rotted away so that he could not be quite certain about the position of 'boat four'. The same year a collection of jewellery from the sword sheaths of officers from a deposition of the 5th century was found by chance in the bog. H. P. Hanssen tried secretly to get the objects to the National Museum in Copenhagen, but this was stopped by the German authorities. This find resulted in German archaeologists from Kiel taking an interest in renewed excavations in the bog. The first attempt in 1893 was made at a position far away from Engelhardt's pit, and nothing was found there. But the archaeologists paid their workmen well, and therefore some of these tried to trace information on the exact position of Engelhardt's finds in order to get new excavations going.

H. P. Hanssen had inherited the patriotic mind of his parents, and he became a famous politician for the Danish minority at the parliament in Kiel 1896-1908 and later at the parliament in Berlin 1906-1919. Now he was faced with the threat that Engelhardt's secret fourth boat should be found by the German archaeologists, and this prospect he could not bear. The plots of land in the bog were owned by various farmers in the area, and even if they were all 'Danish-minded' they could be brought under pressure by the German officials to allow renewed excavation activities in the bog. Therefore H. P. Hanssen very secretly arranged that the plots pointed out by Povl Adam as the

potentially interesting ones were sold by the farmers to a patriotic Danish pharmacist, Chr. Mikkelsen in Odense, Denmark, far out of reach of the Kiel archaeologists. With this move H. P. Hanssen managed to stop this 'threat' to the site.

At the death of Chr. Mikkelsen the Danish National Museum inherited the plots in Nydam Bog. Thus Hanssen and Mikkelsen jointly had tried to arrange for the museum to take responsibility for future excavations to conclude Engelhardt's work, even if the Nydam region at that time was still part of Germany. In the Mikkelsen-case the patriotic attitude was also continued within the family. Thus the son, P. Helweg Mikkelsen, in the 1930s excavated the Viking ship found at Ladby, paid for the construction of a concrete vault over it and transferred the ownership of the site to the National Museum.

H. P. Hanssen lived to see the reunion of the northern part of the Slesvig region with Denmark in 1920, but not to see the National Museum excavating in the Nydam bog. In the meantime a new find had turned up in the small Hjortspring bog on the nearby island Als with early Iron Age weapons and parts of a boat. In 1921-1922 G. Rosenberg from the National Museum carried out the very intricate work of excavating and raising this find, followed by conservation and restoration of the boat in the National Museum in Copenhagen (Rosenberg 1937). In the 1930s Rosenberg was engaged in the excavation of the Ladby Viking ship, and this left no time for concerns about the situation in Nydam.

Finally in 1939 J. Brøndsted and C. J. Becker from the National Museum came to the bog in Nydam. They laid out a grid and excavated a number of test-pits, one of these with a fragment from the broken-up oak boat of which Engelhardt had also found some parts. A few spear shafts were also found, but nothing that seemed to justify any large-scale excavations. The general impression was that Engelhardt's excavation had brought to light, more or less, all finds from the bog. The story of the fourth boat was either not known or not believed at the time. Thus the general analysis of the find by various archaeologists was based on the assumption that the excavated finds could be used to determine the total number of warriors in the armies which had been defeated. In contrast to Engelhardt it could now be established that the finds represented more than one deposition in the bog. There was a clear distinction between older and younger objects, with the 1888 silver objects as the youngest ones, found without contemporary weapons. Thus this deposition was taken to be a *pars pro toto* offering, reflecting a transition of the custom over time.

During the Second World War the Danish bogs were again used for cutting peat for fuel, and this activity produced a large number of finds of logboats in the bogs. Later new sites with large depositions of Iron Age warspoils were found at Ejsbøl and Illerup, and excavated between 1950 and 1985 (Andersen 1956; Ørsnes 1984, 1990; Ilkjær & Lønstrup 1975; Ilkjær 1990). In the 1970s and 1980s work was in progress with the analysis and publication of the Ejsbøl and Illerup finds, and few 'land archaeologists' were tempted at the prospect of a life-long engagement in the Nydam bog to search for a hypothetical boat or to sweep up after Engelhardt, even if his excavation had opened more questions than it had answered.

But for a ship archaeologist Nydam was still the potentially most promising site for anyone in search of fresh evidence of the ships of the Late Roman and Migration Period. Therefore it became a part of the long term research strategy of the Institute of Maritime Archaeology of the National Museum to take up the challenge of continuing Engelhardt's work at Nydam. Quite evidently this should take account of various types of electronic search and probing equipment. A non-destructive survey by these means should be carried out as a basis for possible future excavations in limited areas.

As in all border regions, the interest of history is very vivid in the southern part of Jutland. The events around the Nydam finds have been of strong interest to the people of the region. Therefore in the year of 1983, a "Society for Research of Nydam" was formed on the initiative of local people with the aim of collecting as much information on the famous site as possible. The members of the society worked with different aspects on Nydam: geology, metal detection, studies in archives in Denmark and Germany, etc. Already in February 1984, their work proved fruitful - in a field some 100 m away from the central finding area they detected a number of weapons partly lying so close to the surface that they had been damaged by grazing cows. The new site was reported to the National Museum and an excavation was undertaken in June the same year (Petersen 1987).

The excavation revealed small groups of weapons which had been stuck down into the peat at the edge of the Iron Age lake. The depositions here can be dated to the 5th century which offers a new perspective to the whole Nydam concept. The finds consisted of all the common types of weapons (except axes) whereas no personal equipment or metal work from bandoleers or sword sheaths

were found. As is the case with the high status silver works from sword sheaths found in 1888, the new find contains groups of material sorted out from the total equipment - this time of a more ordinary social frame. The *pars pro toto* theory has to be revised.

Inspired by the local initiative, a research project for Nydam was launched in 1989 by the National Museum. This project is still in progress and the aim is to gain new knowledge on a number of aspects of the site and of the finds. The field research programme is focusing on four main themes. Firstly, to get a complete mapping and dating of the different areas with depositions in the bog. Secondly, to locate and re-excavate the area where Engelhardt found the boats in 1863, attempting to find supplementary boat material. In the third place, to get a view of the state of preservation of the artefacts from the bog and finally by pollen analysis to reconstruct the history of the transformation of the lake into the bog with the development of the surrounding cultural landscape.

Since the start of the project, excavations and investigations have been carried out on several levels. Many different aspects of each main theme have been dealt with, and after the 1992 excavating season the following statement can be given:

After the finds in 1984, it is known that depositions have taken place in an area of minimum 150 m by 100 m and that the actual area might even be larger than estimated today. This stresses the fact that the mapping of the bog by non-destructive methods is important - but also very time consuming. As earlier excavations have shown, the nature of the deposits differ from area to area. Under most circumstances, metal artefacts are found together with wooden objects but there are also locations where only wood is found. These places are typically in the reed zone of the Iron Age lake where floating wood has been caught.

The methods of mapping have been multiple. The surface has been searched with metal detectors while magnetometers have been used for mapping the iron artefacts in the deeper layers. These investigations have not yet been completed but a number of spots have been located with deeply lying artefacts.

In 1990-91, a test square of 2 m x 2 m was excavated at one of the newly located iron concentrations, and this proved to be a very rich deposition of artefacts from 5th century (Bonde *et al.* 1991). A part of a heap of weapons was revealed containing wooden objects - shafts of spears, lances and arrows, bows and shields, a lot of iron artefacts - shield buckles, knives, spear heads, lances and at least 25 swords - and objects of bronze, bone and glass (pl.7.2).

While the iron material can be detected simply by using electronic equipment, it is more exhausting to locate larger wooden artefacts. The method has been the one of probing with a steel rod with which it is possible to penetrate the fairly soft peat and "feel" for harder wood at a depth of 1 - 1.5 m - a horizon where the deposition layer can be expected. The aim has been to locate boat material

- and in 1990 the method proved successful. Two planks from the chopped up oak boat were located, being excavated the following year (pl.7.3).

Both of these planks were made of oak and had ornamented cleats of the same type as seen on the planks found by Engelhardt in 1863. The planks had been deliberately damaged prior to the depositing into the lake, the edges were split off and several axe marks from the destruction of the vessel could be seen on the planks. The largest of the planks is more than 7 m long and 5 pairs of ornamented cleats are preserved on it, and a 6th pair has been chopped off. The average distance between the cleats is 108 cm, and the original width of the plank can be estimated to be approx. 40 cm. Only fragments of the chopped up oak boat have been found till now, however, much may still remain in the bog.

As Engelhardt fled from Flensburg in 1864, his behaviour clearly demonstrated that he did not want to leave any information to the Germans which might be used as a guide to further excavations in Nydam. Neither in the records for the Flensburg Collection nor in his publications on Nydam are precise excavation plans indicated. Because of this lack of information, the excavations taking place while the region was German from 1864 to 1920 led to no major finds. The only important find of this period is the heap of silver sword sheaths found by chance by peat cutters in 1888.

In 1991-92 an effort was made to locate the area where Engelhardt excavated the boats in 1863. A grid of test ditches was laid out, dug down to a depth where undisturbed peat could be separated from layers which had been disturbed by excavation. At the end of the 1992 excavating season a clear picture of Engelhardt's activities could be drawn. A large area - approx. 25 m long and 4 m wide - where the peat had been excavated before - was located, and fragments from the large oak boat were found, i.e. a chopped off cleat and a fragment of a frame.

Parallel to this area, a smaller excavation pit was recognized - approx. 18 m long and 3 m wide - and here fragments of pine planks were found. As Engelhardt wrote that the oak boat and the pine boat were found side by side in 1863, we are sure that the two areas described in fact are the correct boat locations (Engelhardt 1865).

In 1993, excavations of and around the boat area will be initiated which will undoubtedly provide much new information on the 1863 boats and hopefully also lead to the discovery of more boat material.

The recent investigations in Nydam have revealed that the state of preservation of the artefacts is very varying, depending on where in the bog they have been situated. A research project dealing with the physical and chemical influences on the bog has just started and already the alarm clocks have begun ringing. Some of the iron artefacts are very badly preserved, for instance, in a number of cases the arrow tips have only been recognized

as "shadows" at the ends of the shafts, but also heavier objects as for example axe heads can be of a sugar-like consistency. Some of the wooden artefacts show clear signs of dehydration and last but not least, there is a severe threat of destruction by rhizomes of "horse tails". The bog is filled up with these plants and all the wood found has been penetrated by the thick and strong rhizomes. It seems as if the "horse tail"-attack is of a rather new date but this has to be verified by future investigations.

The history of the sacred Iron Age lake and the landscape surrounding it has been the focus of a series of pollen analytical studies carried out in Nydam by the Natural Science Research Unit of the National Museum. The preliminary results point to the bog once being a rather large fresh water lake with a water surface at a height of about 4 m above sea level (Bonde et al. 1991). Engelhardt was of the opinion that the area was once an inlet connected to the sea but the new investigations demonstrate that all the boats had to be transported over land before they were sacrificed in the deepest part of the existing lake. The surrounding landscape was made up of well-cultivated Iron Age fields which stretched right down to the banks of the lake.

Pollen analytical work combined with $C_{14}$-datings and dendrochronology will enable us to get a much more differentiated picture of the agricultural and climatic changes during the centuries when the lake was in use as a religious centre for the inhabitants of the region. How long did the lake exist? Has the water level been artificially raised? What happened in the landscape prior to and after the use of the lake for sacrificial purposes? etc., etc.

The National Museum's Institute of Maritime Archaeology will continue the search for information on the Nydam boats, through the study of Engelhardt's material supplemented by "fresh" material excavated under the new project. The oak boat in Schleswig will be studied in detail as it has already been demonstrated that not all the secrets of this boat were revealed in the first instance. A new plan of the structure of the vessel will be drawn up. Here, for instance, the scarves in the planking found by Bonde during dendro sampling will be recorded (Bonde 1990). The construction of the oak boat has been dated to 310-320 AD and coming analyses will enable us to date the chopped up oak boat and the pine boat in a better chronological frame than is the case just now.

The Nydam story is continuing. Excavations will be carried out at least until 1995 when we hope to have covered the boat area. A lot of exciting questions might find answers during this period, i.e., will stem and stern posts and other missing parts of the pine boat be found? Will newly found parts from the large oak boat in Schleswig enable us to make a more accurate construction plan of the vessel than Åkerlund's? Is there a fourth hitherto unexcavated boat in the bog? etc., etc.

In writing this article, the 1993-excavation has just started. The first boat timber is found - a thwart probably from the large oak boat, and we hope that another chapter can soon be written shedding new light on the Nydam-complex, adding new information on the development of boats and ships in North European Iron Age.

# References

Andersen, Harald, 1956: Afsked med ådalen (Illerup). *Kuml 1956*. Aarhus.

Bonde, Niels, 1990: Dendrochronologisch Altersbestimmung des Schiffes von Nydam. *Offa. Berichte und Mitteilungen zur Urgeschichte, Frühgeschichte und Mittelalterarchäologie, Band 47*. Neumünster.

Bonde, Niels et al., 1991: Jernalderbåde og våbenofre. Nationalmuseets Nydamprojekt. *Nationalmuseets Arbejdsmark* 1991, København.

Crumlin-Pedersen, Ole, 1990: The boats and ships of the Angles and Jutes. *Maritime Celts, Frisians and Saxons* (ed. S. McGrail). CBA Research Report No. 71. London.

Engelhardt, Conrad, 1865: *Nydam Mosefund 1859-1863*. København.

Engelhardt, Conrad, 1866a: *Denmark in the Early Iron Age*. London.

Engelhardt, Conrad, 1866b: Nydamsbaaden og Nordlandsbaaden. En Sammenstilling mellem Oldtidsbaaden og nogle Nutidsbaade. *Aarbøger for Nordisk Oldkyndighed og Historie* 1866. København.

Engelhardt, Conrad, 1867: *Kragehul Mosefund 1751-1865*. København.

Hanssen, H.P., 1925: Oldsagsfundene i Nydam Mose. *Hejmdal* 1925 nr. 110-112. Åbenrå.

Ilkjær, Jørgen & Jørn Lønstrup, 1975: Nye udgravninger i Illerup ådal. *Kuml 1975*. Aarhus.

Ilkjær, Jørgen & Jørn Lønstrup, 1984: Flensborgsamlingens skæbne. *Hikuin* 10. Højbjerg.

Ilkjær, Jørgen, 1990: *Illerup Ådal I. Die Lanzen und Speere*. Jutland Archaeological Society Publication XXV: I. Aarhus.

Petersen, Peter Vang, 1987: Nydam III - et våbenoffer fra ældre germansk jernalder. *Aarbøger for Nordisk Oldkyndighed og Historie*. København.

Rieck, Flemming & Ole Crumlin-Pedersen, 1988: *Både fra Danmarks Oldtid*. Roskilde.

Rosenberg, Georg, 1937: *Hjortspringfundet*. Nordiske Fortidsminder III, 1. København.

Shetelig, Haakon, 1930: Das Nydamschiff. *Acta Archaeologica* Vol. 1. Copenhagen.

Timmermann, G. 1941: Wie das Nydamschiff gebaut wurde. *Mannus* 33. Jahrg. H.1. Leipzig.

Ørsnes, Mogens, 1984: *Sejrens Pris*. Våbenofre i Ejsbøl Mose ved Haderslev. Haderslev Museum.

Åkerlund, Harald, 1963: *Nydamskeppen. En studie i tidig skandinavisk skeppsbygnadskonst*. Göteborg.

# 8

# THE HUMBER WETLANDS PROJECT:
## An Archaeological Assessment of the Humber Basin Lowlands

### *Paul Davies and Robert van de Noort*

Since the discovery by Ted Wright in 1937 of the first Bronze Age boat at the North Ferriby foreshore (Wright and Wright 1939; Wright 1976), archaeological research in the Humber wetlands has been largely characterised by the integration of cultural and environmental aspects of the past. The exceptional organic preservation of archaeological remains in the Humber wetlands had previously yielded important discoveries, including the Brigg raft (Sheppard 1910) and the Holderness crannogs, or lake-side villages (Smith 1911, Varley 1968). The discovery in 1937, however, heralded a new era wherein man in the past was studied in his natural environment. The site at North Ferriby has now been studied for over fifty years (Buckland *et al.* 1990), and research at Brigg (McGrail 1975; 1981), Thorne Moors (Buckland 1979) and the Hasholme boat site (McGrail and Millett 1985; Millett and McGrail 1987) has revealed the potential for such an integrated approach to our heritage.

### The Humber Wetlands Project

This wealth of previous studies and, more importantly, the proven potential of the region for the wetland preservation of archaeological sites and palaeoenvironmental material has led to the creation of the Humber Wetlands Project which currently employs the authors. The project was commissioned and is funded by English Heritage and based in the School of Geography and Earth Resources at The University of Hull. Dr Steve Ellis is the Project Supervisor and the project is chaired by Professor John Coles.

The River Humber drains approximately one-fifth of the surface area of England (Pethick 1990). Toward the River Humber itself there are large areas of low-lying land which presently are, or previously were, extensive coastal, estuarine or freshwater wetlands. The project is mainly concerned with that area adjacent to the Humber which is below 10m OD, the extent of which is shown on figure 8.1. The project covers approximately 330,000 hectares of land situated in the counties of Humberside, North Yorkshire, South Yorkshire, Nottinghamshire and Lincolnshire. Broadly it consists of five distinct physiographic regions: Holderness and the Hull Valley, the Lincolnshire Marshes, the Ancholme Valley, the Vale of York and the Humberhead Levels.

In broad terms the project is concerned with assessing the archaeological and palaeoecological resource of the area and the threats to this resource. It will also produce an advisory report on the archaeological management of the Humber wetlands. The time span is Late Upper Palaeolithic to Post-Medieval inclusive. More specifically, data are being collated under the four general headings detailed below.

1. *Wetland history:* The extant wetlands of the Humber lowlands cover only a fraction of the area that was occupied by wetlands in the past. Large areas of former wetland are now drained and/or warped, producing some of the most fertile agricultural land in the United Kingdom. Past wetlands within the study area largely occurred below 10m OD. An exception are the many former meres of Holderness (Sheppard 1957; Flenley 1990). The present project is concerned with collating and summarising the data relating to the temporal-spatial development of the lowland wetlands over the past 13,000 years, providing an overview of landscape development against which the archaeological distribution can be compared.

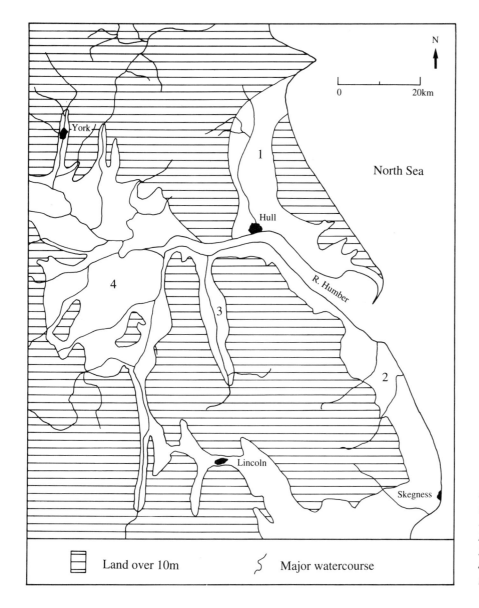

*Figure 8.1 The Humber lowlands.*
*1: Hull valley and Holderness;*
*2: Lincolnshire Marsh;*
*3: Ancholme valley;*
*4: Southern Vale of York and the Humberhead Levels.*

2. *Archaeological sites and finds:* The project is also concerned with mapping archaeological sites and finds which were within or adjacent to those wetlands. Using data from the Sites and Monument Records, the National Archaeological Record and local museums, a database of the sites and finds within this area is being created. The database integrates with a computerised Geographical Information System, on which distribution maps can be plotted according to various criteria (cultural period, site type etc.). This data, in combination with the overview of wetland development will enable consideration of the distribution of sites with respect to the wetland resource as well as the problems of site visibility (known archaeology against potential archaeology).

3. *Wetland preservation potential.* Generally speaking, the post glacial rise in sea-level prompted the aggradation of deep sequences of estuarine and freshwater clays, silts and peats throughout much of the Humber lowlands. Past and present intertidal coastal and estuarine

zones, major and minor river valley bottoms, former meres and the raised mires at Hatfield and Thorne represent areas where aggradation has been greatest and where the possibility of wet-preserved archaeology is high. However, these are also the areas in which archaeology is likely to be least visible. The project aims to identify areas where wet-preserved archaeology may be present and to recommend a strategy whereby this potential can be systematically assessed.

4. *Wetland preservation threats.* Despite the tendency for sediment aggradation through the Flandrian, the wet-preserved archaeology is under continual threat from a number of factors.

Coastal and estuarine margins are subject to erosion. The Holderness coast is disappearing at an estimated rate of two metres per year and many former meres have been completely lost or are currently being rapidly eroded. Within the Humber estuary itself, sites such as North

47

Ferriby would never have been found were it not for tidal scouring. Erosion is thus a double-edged sword for archaeologists, providing both continual opportunity and continual threat.

Drainage of valley bottoms, former meres and raised mires constitutes the most widespread problem for wet-preserved archaeology. Although drainage has been carried out for centuries, the introduction of diesel and electric pumps and an increased demand for arable lands has strongly aggravated the problems caused by artificial drainage. The preliminary data indicate also that the lack of rainfall in the preceding decade has drastically increased the threat, with water tables dropping to unprecedented levels.

Mineral and peat extraction also affects considerable areas of high wet-preservation potential. The archaeological impact of peat extraction at Thorne and Hatfield Moors is comparable to that in the Somerset Levels and the peatlands in the Northwest of England. At Thorne Moor the remains of a Neolithic and early Bronze Age landscape were recently exposed. Sand and gravel extraction in Holderness is also potentially damaging.

General industrial and housing development can threaten wet-preserved archaeology. However, the tendency for major development programmes to concentrate upon existing settlement and industrial locations, most of which do not greatly impinge upon the wetlands, means that the threat is not as severe as those outlined above. A possible exception to this is the planned industrial development of the Humber South Bank.

There are a number of other threats to wet-preserved archaeology which are currently being assessed. These include extensive flood defence work planned for the region, water abstraction programmes and changes in water quality.

## Future Work

The Humber wetlands have to date produced wet-preserved archaeology of a quality comparable to the Somerset Levels and Fenland. However, the remaining wetlands are threatened by drainage, mineral extraction and developments, and the archaeological resource must be considered as a precious reserve which deserves special attention. To create a better understanding of the archaeological remains in the area, an extensive survey of the wetlands is needed; to understand the context of the archaeological remains we should also look at the landscape history and at the occupation of the adjacent higher areas. The survey results can then be used to select the most important archaeological sites and landscapes for active archaeological management. When- and wherever this is possible, the conservation of the archaeological resource should go hand-in-hand with the preservation of the ecological important wetlands (Coles 1984).

## References

Buckland, P.C. 1979. *Thorne Moors; a palaeoecological study of a Bronze Age site*. Birmingham: University of Birmingham, Department of Geography Occasional Paper 8.

Buckland, P.C., Beal, C.J. and Heal, S.V.E. 1990. Recent work on the archaeological and palaeoenvironmental context of the Ferriby Boats. In S. Ellis and D.R. Crowther (eds.), *Humber perspectives: a region through the ages*, 131-46. Hull: Hull University Press.

Coles, J.M. 1984. *The Archaeology of wetlands*. Edinburgh: University Press.

Flenley, J.R. 1990. Vegetational History. In S. Ellis and D.R. Crowther (eds.), *Humber perspectives: a region through the ages*, 43-53. Hull: Hull University Press.

McGrail, S. 1975. The Brigg raft re-excavated. *Lincolnshire History and Archaeology* 10, 5-13.

McGrail, S. (ed.) 1981. *The Brigg 'raft' and her prehistoric environment*. Oxford: National Maritime Museum Archaeological Series No 6, British Archaeological Reports British Series 89.

McGrail, S. and Millett, M. 1985. The Hasholme logboat. *Antiquity* 59, 117-20.

Millett, M. and McGrail, S. 1987. The archaeology of the Hasholme logboat. *Archaeological Journal* 144, 69-125.

Pethick, J.S. 1990. The Humber estuary. In S. Ellis and D.R. Crowther (eds.), *Humber perspectives: a region through the ages*, 54-67. Hull: Hull University Press.

Sheppard, T. 1910. Prehistoric boat from Brigg. *Transactions of the East Riding Antiquarians Society* 17, 33-60.

Sheppard, J. 1957. The Medieval meres of Holderness. *Transactions of the Institute of British Geographers* 23, 75-86.

Smith, R.A. 1911. Lake-dwellings in Holderness, Yorkshire. *Archaeologia* 62, 593-610.

Varley, W.J. 1968. Barmston and the Holderness Crannogs. *East Riding Archaeologist* 1, 11-26.

Wright, E.V. 1976. *The North Ferriby boats: a guidebook*. Greenwich: National Maritime Museum.

Wright, C.W. and Wright, E.V. 1939. Submerged boat at North Ferriby. *Antiquity* 13, 349-53.

**Plate 6.3-6.5**

Pl. 6.3 A collar for a wooden wedge, constructed of twined cedar bough.

0             5

Pl. 6.4 Example of wooden wedges with cordage collars from Hoko River.

Pl. 6.5 Examples of the shredded cedar-bark capes/skirts common to Hoko River. Note bent down selvage with the spruce root string core. Scale cm.

**Plate 7.1**

*Pl. 7.1 The first archaeological investigations in Nydam were carried out in 1859-1863 by the Danish archaeologist Conrad Engelhardt (1825-1881).*

**Plate 7.2-7.3**

*Pl. 7.2 Detail of a heap of war booty excavated in 1990-91 by Peter Vang Petersen from the Danish National Museum. Photo Per Poulsen.*

*Pl. 7.3 The lifting of the large plank from the chopped up oak boat in 1991. Photo Per Poulsen.*

**Plate 10.1-10.3**

Pl. 10.1  Prepatation of a green oak slab, by hollowing it out until the walls are 10mm thick.
Pl. 10.2  The prepared slab set in a jig.
Pl. 10.3  After three hours, the oak slab is fully straightened without cracking.

**Plate 11.1**

*Pl. 11.1  A Hainan trader between Haikou and Zhanjiang. Note the battened fores'l and beneath it the large centreboard.*

**Plate 11.2-11.3**

*Pl. 11.2 Three of 'Waynes 27' – a tiny remnant of China's sailing tradition.*

*Pl. 11.3 A rare site in Amoy today. Note the unsupported mast.*

**Plate 13.1-13.2**

*Pl. 13.1 Porlock Marsh and Porlock Bay, seen from the west. Copyright: Exmoor National Park.*

*Pl. 13.2 Old Burrow Roman fortlet, seen from the air. Copyright: F. M. Griffith, Devon County Council.*

**Plate 15.1-15.2**

*Pl. 15.1 Stempost and garboard planks seams on a Tamil Nadu masula. Note the exceptionally long plugs.*

*Pl. 15.2 Marsula from Orissa with characteristic double web sewing on all seams.*

# 9

# A WINGED CLEAT FROM HARTLEPOOL

## Valerie Fenwick

High up the east coast of England and north of the Humber Estuary where Ted Wright and his brother made such astonishing discoveries, there are further areas of ancient landscape exposed at low water (fig.9.1). To walk across the peat beds of Hartlepool Bay is to be reminded of the remains of Neolithic woodland on the North Ferriby foreshore, so beautifully preserved that its acorns are crunched beneath 20th-century boots. There, too, the horizontal trunks of large oaks lie scattered and scoured by the tide.

The peat beds in Hartlepool Bay are partly overlaid by a thin layer of sand and sea coal dust which local people still collect, although the site has been designated of Special Scientific Interest. There are two levels of peat; the upper has been subject to drying and contains little visible environmental material unlike the lower thicker layer which contains archaeological finds and is related to a brief fall in sea-level about 5000 BP. Thin underlying layers of silt contain microliths (Tooley 1978; Tann 1991). Other local people scan the peat for artefacts. Of these Mr Reg Dowey has reported the most discoveries. During more than twelve years of regular winter searches he found worked flint, bone and Red Deer antler, and in 1972 an associated crouched Neolithic inhumation. These discoveries were concentrated around the mouth of the Newburn Raw where excavation by Cleveland County Archaeology Section in 1990 revealed a line of wooden stakes and Neolithic settlement debris (Tann 1991,15)(fig.9.2).

Also near the mouth of the stream, another local man, Mr K Cook of Seaton Carew, in 1969 spotted a circular wooden object embedded in the peat (NGR:5180 3190). He dug it out and presented it to the Gray Museum together with fragments of wood and what was initially thought to be an attached peg. After the museum decided not to sacrifice the sizeable portion which a radiocarbon date at that time required, conservation and PEG impregnation was carried out by the Area Museum Service.

Fig. 9.1 *1. Hartlepool Bay 2. North Ferriby*

Neither the British Museum nor the Nationalmuseet in Copenhagen was able to provide parallels for the object and it was generally agreed that it was probably a lid for a container of bark or leather. At that time a Mesolithic date was presumed.

## Description

Visual examination suggests that the object is made of oak and was intended to be circular (fig.9.3). Unfortunately no identification of the wood was made prior to conservation and no photographs could be traced in 1993. In correspondence in 1969 the curator, Mr Hackett, reported

49

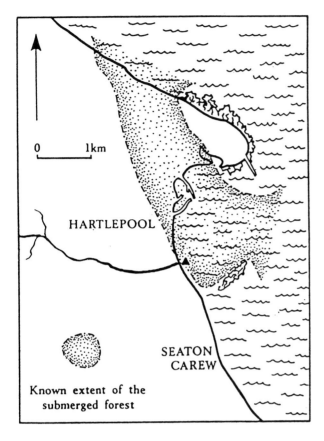

*Fig. 9.2 The known extent of the submerged forest in Hartlepool Bay. The winged cleat was found close to the mouth of the Newburn Raw. Based on a map by Cleveland County Archaeology Section.*

that it was being 'kept in a moist condition', but examination today suggests that a small amount of drying out may have taken place; it measures 188mm along the grain but 5mm less transversely. The maximum thickness is 60mm.

On one side there is a flat nearly circular recess 140 x 135mm and about 10mm deep; on the other a cleat has been formed about 25mm above the surrounding surface. The side of the object is bevelled and there are large facets impinging on the ends of the cleat where the wood has been trimmed. The top of the cleat appears worn and on the other side the upper part of about half the rim is incomplete. The object was broken when found and the longitudinal fracture has been made good with wax. The surface within the cleat is rough and the clearest evidence of working survives at the junction between the rim and the recessed area, where there is a series of toolmarks. These show a straight cutting edge about 17mm long and in places there are toolmarks like knife kerfs as much as 33mm long. On the upper surface of the cleat there are raised rays about 10mm long, while the underside has an area of apparent silver grain. It seems to have been carved from the outer part of a substantial trunk.

Reactions to the 'lid', as it is known, have been those of perplexity. No parallels have been identified and it appears disproportionately heavy for its size. The bevelled

sides suggest that it plugged the mouth of a container; the rim on the other hand suggests that it fitted like a jam jar lid, albeit very inefficiently on account of the sloping profile. Its shape seems more likely to have been the incidental result of reducing the thickness of the wood by hollowing out the underside.

A further puzzle is the rough workmanship visible in places. Most noticeably the cleat is not centred on the 'lid', but is 21mm off-centre laterally and 19mm longitudinally. Large irregular facets around the perimeter impinge on the base of the cleat while the bevelled sides have in places distinct small facets.

In short, internal evidence suggests that the object has been reworked, perhaps cut down from a much larger item. One reader, Ted, will already have intuited that a boat is to follow. After all, he instantly perceived evidence for a fifth boat at Ferriby in part of a cleat which I found on the foreshore there on a visit with him four years ago (Wright, 1990, 3.12A).

The form of the little cleat from Hartlepool resembles the single winged cleat which was carved on the underside of the keel-plank of the most complete vessel found at North Ferriby, F1 (fig.9.4). That cleat measured approximately 30 cm in length; it was 30 cm wide and about 12cm at its narrowest where it rose about 5cm above the surrounding wood. Its perforation was also oval, being about 9cm long and 4cm high. Although the function of the Ferriby cleat remains enigmatic, it does provide a regional and obvious parallel for the cleat from Hartlepool, the

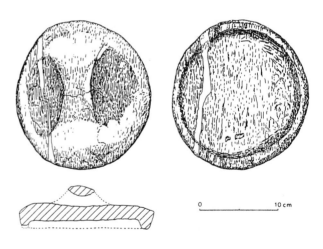

*Fig. 9.3 The wooden 'lid' extracted from the submerged peat in 1969. Drawn in 1993.*

dimensions of which are about one fifth its size. Ferriby 1 is estimated to have originally been about 16m long. If the cleat was indeed salvaged from a comparable vessel, then it can be assumed to have been much smaller.

As a maximum reconstruction of the evidence, and for Ted's divertissement, a little boat about 3m long is here

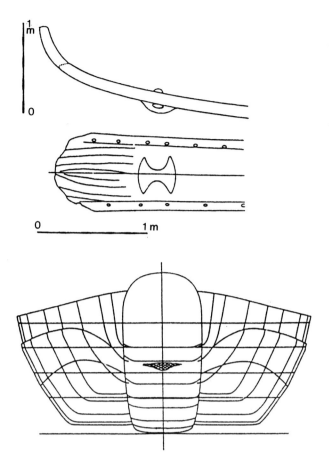

*Fig. 9.4 The winged cleat carved on the underside of Ferriby 1: a) in elevation b) in plan c) superimposed on the reconstructed body plan by J F Coates (after Wright, 1990).*

postulated. Whether it is indeed Neolithic, and thus older than any of the Ferriby finds, we have at present no way of knowing.

*Acknowledgements.* I am grateful to Hartlepool Museums Service for permission to draw and photograph the 'lid' (Acc. no. 97.69; SMR 1592). Colleagues have been most helpful, in particular, Andrew Holley of the Grey Museum, Robin Daniels, Ian Longworth, Béat Arnold, Richard Darrah, Alison Gale and Hazelle Page.

## References

Tann, G.1991. Research on Hartlepool submerged forest. *Archaeology North* 1,15-16.

Tooley, M.J.1978. The history of Hartlepool Bay. *Int. J. Naut. Archaeol.* 7.1, 71-75.

Wright, E.V.1990. *The Ferriby Boats. Seacraft of the Bronze Age.* London.

# 10

# EXPANDING OAK LOGBOATS-
# IS IT POSSIBLE?

## *Edwin Gifford*

At the conference on Medieval Archaeology in York in 1992, Dr William Filmer-Sankey gave an informal presentation of his recent excavation of an Anglo-Saxon boat grave at Snape, Suffolk. The shape of the marks left in the sand indicate that it might have been an expanded logboat similar to some of those from Slusegard, Bornholm, described by Dr Ole Crumlin-Pedersen (Andesen, Lind and Crumlin-Pedersen 1991), who considers that expansion of such oak logboats is possible. "Oak is considered by many to be unsuitable for expansion. Freshly cut oak is, however, easy to hew to shape and stretch into form. Old craftsmen call it butter oak in contrast to the harder and stiffer bone oak, which results from drying. Oak is not so extremely plastic as aspen, which has been used in recent times for expanded logboats (*espinger*), but using freshly cut oak, a skilled builder can certainly make this type of boat". Wood fibres found in the Snape grave are at present being analysed to determine the species.

## Purpose of Test

Although there is extensive evidence of contemporary expanded logboats, these are thought to be limited to soft woods (using obeche in West Africa and aspen in Finland, for instance). Doubts have been expressed about the practicality of bending oak across the grain in this manner, as this would put tensile stresses on the medullary rays, which make oak wood particularly susceptible to splitting. Therefore, the following tests have been made.

## Tests

The first test was simply exploratory. A straight section of plank 300 x 150 x 28mm was cut from green oak slab wood. Although this was not fully representative of the curved dugout section, it was suitable for a first approxi-

mation. The sample was set in a jig fitted with two loading screws, immersed in hot water and slowly bent over a period of 40 hours, by which time a radius of 700mm had been achieved before failure occurred. This result was encouraging.

Then it was learned that seven iron pins 8-10mm long had been found near the bottom of the Snape boat, which indicate a possible thickness. Logboats with a similar dimension have been found in Oceania and one example can be seen in the Exeter Museum. So a second test was made of a 10mm straight section cut from the same slab. After only three and a half hours of heating, it had been bent to a radius of 300mm before failure, a great improvement.

If a straight piece of plank cut tangentially from the side of a log could be bent to a radius of 300mm, then it seemed likely that a curved circumferential section cut from a log of 300mm radius could be straightened out. So for a final test, a curved section 10mm thick was cut from the outer hardwood layers of a green oak 600mm diameter log (pl.10.1). This was set in the jig (pl.10.2) and fully straightened, without failure, after only three hours in hot water (pl.10.3); an astonishing and convincing demonstration of the bending capacity of butter oak. After careful drying, the sample converted to bone oak and retained its straightness.

These tests demonstrate that green oak can be substantially bent (or straightened) across the grain after a relatively short period in hot water. As the deformations obtained in the tests are so much greater than would be required in boat building, by a factor of at least two, further investigation is justified. Drawings of the Snape find are not yet available, so use has been made of a hypothetical cross-section such as might result from an actual expansion in order to make some simple calculations of stability for this type of boat.

A contemporary method of expansion is to set up the green logboat above a slow charcoal fire and partly fill it with hot water, which can be kept hot by adding stones heated in the fire. Gradual outward pressure is applied to the sides of the boat by wedged struts. As most of the bending takes place in that part of the boat actually heated, the greatest effect is likely to be in the bottom water-filled area while the upper parts may retain the original curvature. The shape resulting from this differential expansion (fig.10.1), has a relatively flat bottom and should therefore have better stability than a simple round shape. Indeed preliminary analysis of a 4m long boat with this mid-ship shape shows that it would be stable with four men without need for ballast, with a freeboard of 170mm, and perhaps within the carrying capacity of two strong men.

*Further Work*

The next step is to cut a half-metre long mid-ship section and to expand this in the manner previously described. A

system of flexible bulkheads has been devised to contain the hot water whilst the boat is expanded. On satisfactory completion of this stage, a full-size craft could be built when the drawings of the Snape boat become available. For the present however, it must be realised that these tests are few and simple, and the shape predicted is hypothetical. It remains to be seen whether sufficient skills can be acquired to translate the theory into a boat.

*Postscript*

Since writing this note the author has seen the drawings of Snape '91 which show a remarkable coincidence between the midship section of the grave-boat and the hypothetical expansion described in this paper. The only significant difference is that the actual boat is smaller (being 2.90 x 0.5 x 0.25m) and the carrying capacity is therefore approximately half that of the hypothetical boat.

Reference

Andesen, S., Lind, B. and Crumlin-Pedersen, O. 1991. *Boat-graves and grave-boats at Slusegard*. Aarhus.

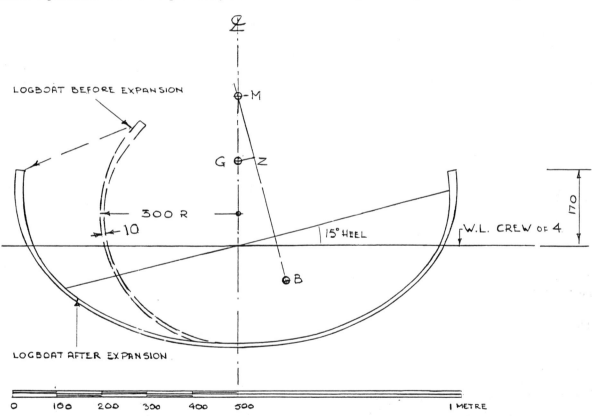

*Fig. 10.1 Hypothetical expansion of a 4 metre logboat.*

53

# 11

# THE SLOW BOATS OF CHINA
## Boat Hunting in the People's Republic

## *David Goddard*

The International Sailing Craft Association is a charity dedicated to finding and preserving the world's traditional working craft propelled by oar and sail. China, probably the world's most boat-dependent country, is poorly represented in its collections, and in 1990 the Winston Churchill Memorial Trust offered it the chance to put this right. It gave the Association's Director, myself, a travelling fellowship to study the traditional boats of China.

China is a vast place from which little information escapes and even the Chinese seem to know little of their maritime and riverine cultures which is surprising since the boat is commoner than the car. Even the smallest stretch of water will be inhabited by some form of boat and that boat is quite likely to be a masterpiece of sophisticated simplicity, of brilliant low tech.

The first visit of my wife and myself had to be to Peking to meet the Institute of Navigation, to whom I had been writing for half a year in the hope that they might point us in the right directions. They were excellent hosts but knew nothing of boats that were blown by the wind.

We were to discover that the Cultural Revolution had brain-washed people to feel that the use of wind was decadent and a matter of shame. We launched ourselves at the first objective, the island of Hainan, the largest of China's off shore islands and the most southerly. Here we found the biggest fleet of sailing traders in the world. The boats could be seen from the air as we came in to land at the capital Haikou and in the creek that afternoon we found more than fifty two- and three-masted junks. The hulls were more Arab than Chinese, being long and graceful, but the rudders were vast and fenestrated and they all carried huge centreboards operated by their own hand winches (pl.11.1).

The particular characteristic of these Hainan traders is the battened jib, the peak of which runs up to the top of the mainmast. Many were over 30m long, crewed entirely by men - they were not family boats - and it seemed that most of their trade was in carrying bulk loads, building materials particularly, between Hainan and the port of Zhanjiang on the mainland to the North.

Later on, after an uninformative sally to the south of the island, we took the ferry to Zhanjiang. Here we saw buoys of netted, expanded polystyrene the size of small cars, supporting fish-nets. These were being dragged beneath the surface by the force of the tide. Shortly afterwards we sailed right through a fleet of twenty of those magnificent traders. Whether they had been waiting for the tide to change, or through a desire for comradeship, they must have started at the same time and were still close enough together to present a memorable spectacle, unique in the late twentieth century.

Zhanjiang itself was a disappointment boat-wise, the highlight being a visit to a brand new and very beautiful hotel opened only the day before with eight hours of continuous merciless firecracker. The ferry back to Haikou was cancelled; there was not enough water to get out of the harbour and it nearly failed the next day when the skipper's greedy desire to squeeze on one more lorry caused a jam. He missed the morning tide but, allowing the wind to blow the ship across the offending sandbank, he just made it in the afternoon. From Haikou we flew back to Hong Kong, recuperated and prepared for the next sally - to Xiamen, better known as Amoy.

Xiamen was a day and a night away by ferry and a boat enthusiast in our embassy in Peking had told us that it was dead so far as sail was concerned, and he was very nearly right. But within an hour of arriving in our hotel room, overlooking the water, a splendid old lady of about 20m went by, propelled only by those sails that appear to be quilted (pl. 11.3). Her oculus looked forward which some would say distinguished her from a fishing boat, whose eyes look down. This is a myth. We were to see only one more of the 20m craft, even older, and although we went by boat round various corners and islands we could not find their destination and of course no-one would tell us.

It was now time to venture inland to the lakes that cling to the Yangtze. We decided upon Donting Hu the most up-river of the three great lakes, and the town of Yueyang on its eastern shore seemed a good base. It was far from beautiful. The little pagoda emerged from the ubiquitous pile of rubbish and the Chinese equivalent of buddleia sprouted from every layer. The fish market was more promising but there was no sign of sail. Apart from the tiniest boats, which were rowed, all were propelled by smoky, noisy diesels but undoubtedly the hulls were still of ancient lineage. Once again no-one admitted to the presence of sail and they seemed to be right until, having lunch in the hotel on the third day, we saw way off on the horizon, a group of tall rectangles that could only be the sails of a fishing fleet. But no-one could tell us where they came from or where they were going. It seemed that the only way to discover more was to take the ferry round and across the lake on a two day trip to Chagde. But we never made Chagde, the water in the river was too low. We were asked to transfer to a smaller boat but we baulked. The fishing fleet would not be right up a shallow river so we stayed on the bigger boat and returned to Yueyang. The lake had its interests. There were many small fleets of fishing sampans rafted together in the evenings, presumably into family or tribal groups. The water was thick with mud and very shallow but we were lucky enough to see a small school of the world's rarest cetaceans - the Yangtze dolphin. It also changed our luck.

On our return to the hotel we met three Englishmen in the lift. That was a surprise because Yueyang was no place for a holiday and did not seem to offer much by way of business. But business it was. The British were building a coal-fired power station not 8 km away. It took a while for the penny to drop but drop it did... If the British were building a power station, they would be bringing in 12 m containers full of equipment and shipping them back empty. We seized the opportunity and after lengthy negotiations with many helpful people we arranged to buy two sampans and have them delivered to the British for shipment to England. It worked and there are now in Exeter Maritime Museum a fisherman's and a fish merchant's sampan, the latter is 11 m long and very beautiful.

We also found the fishing fleet. It appeared one evening on a sand-spit on an island about 5 km away. There were about fifteen boats, 18 m long with high rectangular many-battened sails. They were family homes and the smoke curling from their cooking fires presented a grand old-world scene - but they were all made of ferro-cement and their hulls were no more than lumps of ugly concrete.

During these expeditions a friend, Wayne Moran, had been sailing down the coast of China from Shanghai to Hong Kong and reported seeing two small fleets of fishing junks still operating under sail. The larger fleet, some 27 boats in all, he said, came from the heavily indented coast about 60 km south of Jiaojiang. They came to be known as 'Wayne's 27' and were to be target of the next sortie.

We flew to Shanghai, spent one night there and caught the afternoon ferry to Jiaojiang arriving there the following morning. We immediately found a small collection of very run-down junks in a muddy creek just outside the town but, since, unlike 'Wayne's 27', their sails were not painted they could not be his.

After various adventures with a hired car of unreliable disposition and frustrating detours we finally found the fleet. Their sails (pl.11.2) were painted, there were twenty nine of them and their hulls were exactly those of Wayne's photograph. We photographed everything and as the light failed set off again in the cramped little waggon, back to Jiaojiang. The journey back to Shanghai, by road and rail because the wind was too much for the ferry, brought home the last dreadful truth.

For nearly 350 km of train journey we were seldom out of sight of water and all Chinese water is boat-infested. We must have seen over two thousand boats, from tiny sampans to great hay-carrying barges that had completely vanished beneath their hay-stack cargoes. It would probably be an exaggeration to say that perhaps fifteen out of all the boats we saw were made of wood, the rest were of concrete, or, in a few cases, of steel.

A month later, and after a sorti into North Vietnam - a very different story - the Director of ISCA, for the first time alone, took the ferry to the east from Hong Kong, to the busy fishing port of Shangwei. There he found Wayne's second fleet, a grand collection of three-masted junks. There were no more than thirty of them in a port that contained a thousand boats. They were old and their hulls were tatty. They were trawlers with a windlass that reached right across the boat. They were fishing machines not homes, except the cockroaches. Their rudders were atypical being deep and narrow, but they were genuinely beautiful and certainly worthy of saving.

The sad conclusion from all these experiences is simple enough. A country that has seen the greatest diversification and the most universal use of water transport, where age is still revered, has no regard for these artefacts of their great civilisation, unless of course they can be used as a tourist attraction. They have salvaged and preserved an ancient wreck because it seemed fashionable but all the rest have vanished without trace. This trait and the 'shame factor' have resulted in the almost total loss of all the wonderful boats that once graced China. A few remnants remain and it is the aim of the International Sailing Craft Association to reach out and save just a few more.

# 12

# A SIDE RUDDER FROM THE LONDON WATERFRONT

## Damian Goodburn

Although Ted Wright is not personally active in urban waterfront excavation he has been a formative influence on all the archaeology of the mud zone - between dry land and water. His pioneering work at North Ferriby has encouraged others to examine Britain's foreshore zone for its undoubted archaeological potential. His publications on the Bronze Age Ferriby boats have proved invaluable during urban waterfront excavations in Dover. Here the field archaeological team was able to recognise the importance of a few scraps of waterlogged timber, and with the help of Ted Wright and others excavate a Bronze Age boat-find of world significance.

The waterlogged zones along the Thames and its tributaries have yielded a number of relatively complete Roman and later boat-finds (Marsden 1981; Marsden ed. 1989) and a vast corpus of fragmentary nautical finds (Goodburn 199; Goodburn in press). Unfortunately, despite several decades of work along London's waterfronts no prehistoric planked boats have been found. The fragmentary finds from London date from Roman times to the 18th century, and derive from vessels of many different types. Most of this material has been excavated and recorded by archaeological teams from the Museum of London as part of rescue archaeology projects. A small number of these timbers have been selected by the museum for conservation, including the two dealt with here. This paper will briefly discuss one particularly unusual find of an oak side rudder or steering oar dating to about AD 1000.

## The circumstances of discovery

The Museum of London's Department of Urban Archaeology carried out a series of rescue excavations, watching briefs and a large scale stopping brief on a redevelopment site, Vintners Place, at the NW end of Southwark Bridge. The stopping brief arrangement between the building and archaeological teams allows a watching brief to be maintained and when high priority areas are exposed the ground works can be halted and rapid excavation and recording of structural remains take place. Although far from ideal, it was possible for the field team led by D.Malt, R.Brown and D.Lees to obtain a fairly reliable coverage of the whole site (Brown and Lees, unpub.). Additionally, it was possible to recover selected timbers of particular interest for detailed recording, sampling and occasionally for preservation.

Reused nautical timbers found on the site include: two sections of different keels; a varied selection of clinker boat planking; a fragment of boat stem and two parts of the side rudder discussed here (fig.1, Goodburn in press).

## Side rudders in general

Side rudders are also loosely known as steering oars, or quarter rudders. Specialised side rudders are known from Roman times and earlier (McGrail 1987,244-251). In the late-Saxon or Viking period they had developed a typical balanced form requiring modest effort to operate. The sailing trials of Viking ship replicas show how effective they must have been at all but very slow speeds. They were flexibly fastened against a curved fulcrum block (wart). They were turned to direct the course of a vessel by a short beam (tiller) passed through their upper ends.

Apparently such rudders were gradually phased out as they were replaced by centre-line stern rudders (also known as median, or axial rudders) in NW European

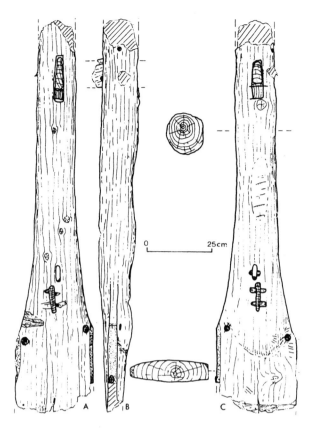

*Fig.12.1 Details of the main body of the two-piece side rudder from Vintners' Place. A) The probable inboard face, tiller socket uppermost, B) Side view, sapwood stippled, C) Outboard view showing hewn flat on shaft, blocked attachment holes and faint axe marks.*

vessels from the late 12th century onward (McGrail 1987,251). Interestingly, side rudders have rarely been found with ancient shipwreck finds; sometimes they may have been salvaged, on other occasions they must have broken free and drifted away. Side rudders were also easily removed and reused. Waterfront excavations in Bergen recovered five side rudders, or fragments thereof, reused in building foundations (Christensen 1985,152). In the ritualised context of pagan ship-burial, side rudders have been found, as at Gokstad and Oseberg.

Although the Vintners' Place rudder is far from complete we might suggest that it has features of a medium-sized side rudder, perhaps somewhere in between the Oseberg ship's single piece rudder and the largest two-piece rudder from Bryggen (Christensen 1985, 229). The Bryggen example also had a cross-shaped recess around its principal pivot point. This side rudder must have been used on a medium-sized or moderately large vessel for the period.

## Other British side rudder finds

Currently three other British finds of side rudders are known, all found by fishermen off the coast of SE England. Two of these came from near Southwold in Suffolk (Hutchinson 1986), and one from near Rye in Sussex (Marsden 1992,126). Radiocarbon dates place the two Suffolk finds in the period 9th to 11th centuries, and the

Rye find between c. 1150 and 1250 (Marsden 1992,127). Unfortunately none of these finds has been published in any detail, but the Suffolk rudders were 3.91m, and 4.36m long and of a rather narrow-bladed form. The Rye rudder was much larger, with a total length of 6.7m implying use in a very large high-sided vessel.

### The Vintners' Place side rudder

*Dating.* As can be seen from figures 12.1 and 12.2 the Vintners' Place side rudder was cut up for reuse and two of its main components separated. However, they were found adjacent to each other in dumps forming crude timber-laced river embankments (Lees and Brown unpub.). The tree-ring dated stratigraphic sequence suggests that the timbers would have been deposited between AD 1025 and 1060 (Hibberd unpub.). The two side rudder timbers were examined for tree-ring dating but were not thought suitable due to rapid parent tree growth and low number of rings (Ian Tyers pers comm.). It is clear that the rudder had considerable use before deposition thus we might suggest a construction date of c. AD 1000 to 1050. We have no way of knowing if the rudder was constructed locally or derived from a foreign vessel. Additionally there are no stylistic features which can be used to assist in provenancing it.

*Description.* The main body of the rudder (timber VRY89 [5541] ) had been clearly crosscut for reuse with an axe while the rounded shaft end had been truncated by the excavation machine. Its surviving length is 1.47m; perhaps originally this would have been between 3.5 and 4.5m. The top of the blade was 310mm wide and 110mm thick, with the cylindrical shaft having a diameter of 150mm. The end of the rounded shaft, clearly the upper end in use, is pierced by a through mortice that had been recut; it contains the remains of an ash wedge and the end of the tiller (not oak, or ash, but species not yet identified). The broken stub of the tiller is pierced by a 25mm diameter oak peg (fig.12.1). Just above this the shaft itself is pierced by a similar oak peg. Unfortunately it was not possible to sample, for species identification, all the fittings of the rudder timbers prior to conservation and the rudder parts are now temporarily inaccessible. However, some identifications were made in the field and these are noted where appropriate.

Lower down the shaft, where it would have been fastened to the hull fulcrum, there are three strange cross-shaped indentations with central perforations. Two of these had been blocked by a single radially-cleft oak wedge. The small oval mortise that was almost open had a sliver of oak in it. Slightly lower down the rudder two 25mm diameter holes had been bored and fragments of roundwood were found in them, wedged in place with slivers of oak. Towards the bottom of the blade the shank of a square iron nail was found. The narrower, probable trailing edge, is pierced by a 25mm diameter ash peg, which had clearly acted to join another timber to the side rudder blade.

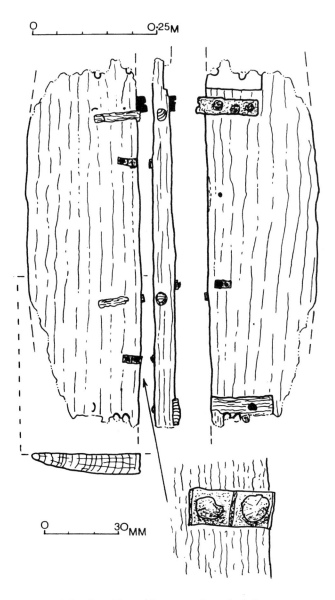

0 _____ 0.25M

0 _____ 30MM

*Fig.12.2 The side rudder extension plank from Vintners' Place, showing edge pegs, wooden and iron straps and nails; also detail of rove strip used as a repair strap.*

*The rudder extension fin.* This radially cleft oak plank fragment (VRY89 [5737]) had been broken at both ends in antiquity, and appeared to have been heavily eroded in use, but it was solid and the iron fittings attached to it little corroded (fig.12.2). The plank is wedge-shaped in cross section and is 0.74m long, 230mm wide and 45mm thick. It has two shallow rectangular recesses cut into one face, each pierced by two small treenail holes. In one recess there are the remains of a thin batten of ash partly secured by a small flat-headed iron nail, the tip driven back into the other face of the timber. The remains of a broken iron strap about 30mm x 3mm, held in place by three flat-headed iron hooked nails, were also found. Both faces had evidence of two further very small and unusual iron straps, each held in place by two small flat headed iron nails. Surprisingly these narrow iron strips were cut with deep grooves running across their width, and were clearly rove strips. Roves for clinker boat rivets were made in strips

pre-cut for easy use, by breaking across the grooves (fig.12.2 detail). Several of these strips have been found on contemporary foreshores in London. Finally, the thicker edge was pierced by two 25mm diameter ash treenails.

It is clear that all these fittings and fastenings had functioned to hold this timber edge-wise to another timber i.e. the side rudder itself. However, it is also clear that it could not have joined the surviving main body of the rudder but must have joined it lower down, where the blade became thinner and wider (fig.12.3a and b). Several of these fittings must have been repairs and their variety and duplication implies repair over a considerable period of time.

*The raw materials used.* The main body of the side rudder had been hewn from a reasonably straight but slightly knotty oak log, and some sapwood was left along part of the top of the blade area, suggesting that a log about 0.45m had been used. The oak from which it was cut had grown fairly fast and was less than 70 years old. Using this information, the grain patterns and an assumption that the form of the rudder was broadly similar to others of the same period in NW Europe, we can tentatively reconstruct the parent tree from which the shaft was cut (fig.12.3c). Oaks of this type can still be found in medieval style coppice with standards woodland; they are not typical of dense high forest or open land oaks. The fin plank was too small to allow its parent tree to be reconstructed but it was clearly radially cleft from a moderately straight, fast grown, oak log over 0.5m in diameter.

## Toolmarks, tool kits and clues about how the rudder was originally made

Wear had removed most of the tool marks, but a few traces were found (fig.12.1), suggesting the use of a number of tools. Most of the marks appear to have been made during the repair or modification of the rudder. For brevity the marks actually found are listed here:

1. Faint axe or adze incut marks survived, on the curved bossed side of the rudder which indicates the use of notch and chop technique for the original hewing of this timber.

2. The rounded shaft had faint, slightly curved, axe stop-facets 70mm long in a flatted area which appeared to be a modification.

3. There were axe incut marks in the area of the tiller wedge and the blocked cross-shaped recesses, the longest of which was 75mm long.

4. The ragged axe-cut fin end had clear axe facets, similar to the above. Indeed, it is likely that all these marks were made by similar axes with blades about 75mm wide. This would be commensurate with those of a Wheeler Type I general purpose woodsman's axe (Wheeler 1927). This type of axe was probably also used for felling the two different oaks used.

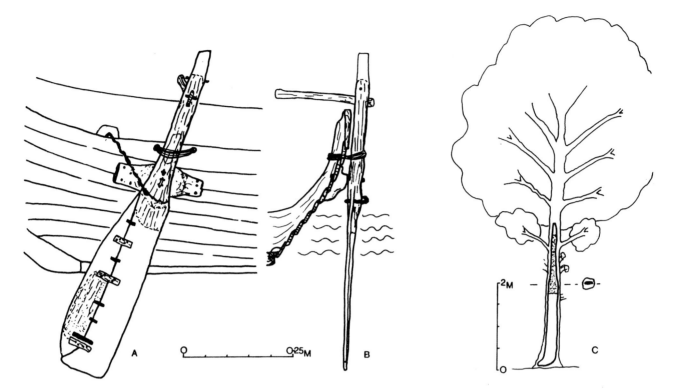

*Fig.12.3 A) Reconstruction side elevation diagram showing how the two parts of the Vintners' Place side rudder probably would have articulated in use on the stern quarter of a medium sized to large vessel, B) A hypothetical side view of same, C) Diagram to show the hypothetical type of parent oak used for the main body of the side rudder.*

For the list above several other tools can be deduced; two sizes of auger, 25mm and about 18mm in diameter, both for boring the round holes and for boring the ends of the oval mortices; a chisel type tool for cutting the recesses; a hammer for driving the nails; an awl for starting them; poles for supporting the rudder parts during construction. It is likely that the rudder fin was trimmed with a broad-bladed axe, the marks of which are common on such cleft planking at this period (Goodburn 1992,112). A draw knife or shave may also have been used to smooth and round some parts of the rudder. All of these tools would have been basic parts of a contemporary boatbuilder's tool kit.

*Evidence of how the Vintners' Place side rudder was attached.* The main pivot point of the rudder was clearly through the small cross-shaped recessed hole (fig.12.3a and b). The linkage may have been secured by a locking pin that passed through a hole in it, at right angles, hence the cross-shaped recess. The two 25mm diameter holes containing wedged fragments of roundwood are suggestive of the use of a twisted withy loop of some type. Perhaps this was for the attachment of a safety line for use if the main linkage broke or for adjusting the rudder during beaching.

## Wider interpretations of the evidence of repair, refastening and wear of the side rudder

It is clear that the mortice for the tiller had been moved up once and the main pivot point moved up twice (fig.12.1). The shaft of the rudder had also been trimmed after

original shaping. This suggests trial and error modification of the rudder or, perhaps less likely, the transfer of the rudder to another vessel.

The multitude of edge fastenings and straps that were used to tie the fin to the main body of the rudder showed that it had a repeated tendency to come adrift in use. The original fastenings were perhaps the edge pegs and the recessed wooden straps, the metal straps being later repairs. The choice of the very weak pre-cut rove strips is clearly very inappropriate, and has to be explained. It is probable that this phase of repair was carried out, either at a remote landing place without materials or facilities for smithing, or perhaps even at sea. It is probable that rove strips were carried by a well-equipped large vessel, together with a basic tool kit to deal with running repairs.

Side rudders were in some ways the most complex fittings of the vessels of the time and as such store considerable information about maritime tradition and life. A thorough review of these finds is therefore long overdue. Hopefully this paper made a small contribution to understanding one of the subtler and most mysterious aspects of the medieval shipwright's craft.

*Acknowledgements.* Without the keen eyes and hard work of the Vintners' Place excavation team this rare find would not have been made. S.Ganon assisted with the recording and D. Lees kindly read a draft of this text, but any remaining errors are the author's.

*Damian Goodburn*

## References

Brown, R. and Lees, D. unpub. Vintners' Place site archive report, Museum of London.

Christensen, A. 1985. Boat finds from Bryggen. In A. Herteig (ed) *The Bryggen papers*. Main series vol.1, 47-278. Bergen: Universitets Forlaget.

Goodburn, D. 1991. New light on early ship and boatbuilding in the London area. In G.Good, R.Jones and M.Ponsford (eds), *Waterfront archaeology: proceedings of the third international conference, Bristol 1988*, 105-111. CBA Research Report No.74.

Goodburn, D. 1992. Wood and woodland; carpenters and carpentry. In G. Milne *et al.*, *Timber building techniques in London c.900-1400*, 106-131. London and Middlesex Arch Soc. Special Paper No. 15.

Goodburn, D. in press, Anglo-Saxon boat finds from London: are they English? In *Procs. 6th International symposium on ship and boat archaeology*, Roskilde 1991.

Hibberd, H. 1993 unpub. Tree ring and wood ID. report for Vintners' Place, Museum of London archive report.

Hutchinson, G. 1986, The Southwold side rudders. *Antiquity* 60, 219-221.

Marsden, P. 1981. Early shipping and the waterfronts of London. In G. Milne and B. Hobley (eds) *Waterfront archaeology in Britain and northern Europe*, 10-16. CBA Research Report No. 41.

Marsden, P. (ed) 1989. A late-Saxon logboat from the London borough of Hackney. *Int. J. Naut. Archaeol.* 18:2, 89-111.

Marsden, P. 1992. Roman and medieval shipping of S.E. England. In *Medieval Europe 1992, Maritime studies, ports and ships*, 125-130.

McGrail, S. 1987. *Ancient boats in North West Europe*. London, Longman.

Wheeler, M. 1927. *London and the Vikings*. London Museum catalogue No.1.

# 13

# A PERSPECTIVE FROM PORLOCK :
## The Maritime Potential of the Exmoor Coast

## *Veryan Heal*

Exmoor lies across the border between North Devon and West Somerset (fig.13.1); its landscape includes upland heather and grass moorland, coastal heath, valley and coastal woodland, farmland and precipitous cliffs. Though best known for its population of ponies and red deer and for the legend of Lorna Doone, Exmoor also represents an untapped archaeological resource. Perhaps due to the proximity of Dartmoor, with its impressive granite monuments, the organic wealth of the Somerset Levels and the alluring abundance of Wessex, Exmoor's archaeology has largely been overlooked, by-passed by antiquaries and archaeologists. Apart from apparent, but unrecorded, 'openings' of barrows and occasional field excursions by local archaeological societies, comparatively little attention has been paid to a landscape which is laden perhaps more subtly, with the evidence of human exploitation over millennia. Agricultural practices of recent decades have taken their toll, not only on the richer soils of the valleys, but also on moorland and heath drained and ploughed to the very edge of the cliffs, yet there remains a wide range of field evidence awaiting proper consideration, investigation and protection.

In order to address this, Exmoor National Park Authority took its first archaeologist on to the staff in 1991. With a background in maritime archaeology and having earned her waterwings and mud-shoes on the foreshore at North Ferriby in the inspiring company of Ted Wright, that archaeologist had no hesitation in identifying the maritime potential of the 29 miles of coast which form the northern boundary of the National Park from Combe Martin in the west to Minehead in the east. This contribution, written as archaeological surveys are getting underway inland and on the coast, explores some of the known evidence for activity in the maritime zone of Exmoor and represents initial thoughts as to how the potential of the area could be exploited, bringing together prehistoric and historic evi-

dence for the use of the foreshore, shore and immediate hinterland and for the role played by the coastal resources in the economic life of past communities on Exmoor.

The geology of Exmoor consists principally of Devonian sandstones, slates and shales, with occasional silaceous limestone (Curtis 1971). None of these rocks provide good or durable building stone, a factor in the resultant small scale of lithic monuments on Exmoor. The underlying rocks have weathered to form a landscape of wide summits intersected by steep combes and river valleys. Quaternary deposits, including blanket peats, overlie the rock and soils range from free draining loam over clay in the fertile lower lands, to gleys and iron pans beneath peat in the uplands. The land mass slopes down from north-west to south-east and is edged by some of the highest cliffs in England, rising to 1500 feet. For seafarers it is not a friendly coast, but there are a few small harbours, at Combe Martin, Lynmouth and Porlock Weir, various usable inlets, as at Heddon's Mouth and beaches, usually of large pebbles, occasionally of sand, at the foot of steep cliffs, as at Embelle or Sillery. From the higher points inland and from the clifftops, the coast of South Wales and the islands of Lundy, Flat Holm and Steep Holm are visible across the difficult waters of the Bristol Channel.

During the last glaciation the area now known as Exmoor lay beyond the southern edge of the ice sheets. With their retreat c. 8,300 BC forest vegetation developed and during the seventh millennium BC sea level rose in the lower Severn Valley, flooding valleys, submerging vegetation and creating salt marshes and mud flats (Aston and Burrow 1982, 15). In the intertidal zone at Porlock Weir and Minehead submerged forest remains overlain by blue clay and peat are visible. At Porlock, oak, ash alder, hazel and yew, rooted in 'angular detritus', were noted by Boyd Dawkins in 1865 and worked flint and chert were recov-

## EXMOOR NATIONAL PARK

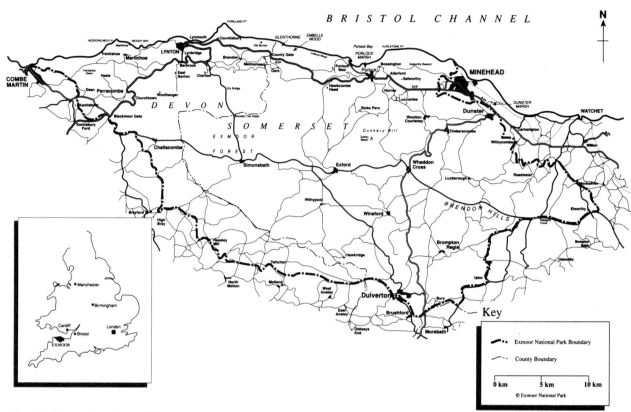

*Fig. 13.1 Location Map of Exmoor*

ered from the 'ferruginous' upper level of the detritus (Boyd Dawkins 1870, 141-142). Some five kilometres up the valley of Hawkcombe, which runs inland from Porlock, large quantities of later mesolithic flints have been found near the spring at Hawkcombe Head over the last fifty years (Aston and Burrow 1982, 20). These microliths of beach pebble flint, probably from Barnstaple Bay some 40 km to the west, are considered to represent four summer hunting camps, used by mesolithic communities who lived in the coastal zone of Porlock at other times of the year (*ibid.*).

Further fieldwork may well produce more mesolithic sites in the coastal and foreshore area of Exmoor, the finds from Porlock and Hawkcombe Head point to systematic seasonal exploitation of resources in different ecozones. Since there is no local source of flint on Exmoor, the means by which it was obtained and identification of the place of origin also needs investigation. The results of such work should throw light on distances travelled or exchange mechanisms.

In the Porlock Bay area, the incentive for investigation is increased by the existence, behind the pebble ridge which marks high water, of an area of former wetland, Porlock Marsh (pl.13.1). Though now cultivated, this flat area, running inland to the gentle rise on which Porlock is built, was water meadow in 1870 (Boyd Dawkins *op.cit.* 141) and still retains a fine duck decoy. The submerged forest levels of the foreshore were surveyed by the RCHME

in the autumn of 1991 and gave levels of -1.9m to -4m OD; they ran back under the seaward edge of the pebble ridge. There is great potential for their preservation beneath the ridge and further inland in the Marsh, where they may continue, overlain by subsequent deposits built up behind the ridge. If this area behind the ridge contains well-preserved sediments considerably more could be learnt about the succession there, whether there were phases of marsh and open water, for example. The likelihood of human exploitation of such a rich environment for game and plant materials is considerable, with the additional possibility of preservation of artefacts and structures associated with hunting, fishing and water transport accumulated over a long period of time.

The Vale of Porlock, which extends inland from Porlock, is famous for its malting barley, a product of the rich soil of the Vale. The combination of the Marsh and fertile arable land would provide an attractive prospect for communities practising agriculture as well as exploiting the naturally occurring resources of the wetland.

When the foreshore exposures were surveyed in 1991, samples were also taken of the forest deposits, the peat and clay. These samples are the first element of a palaeoenvironmental survey of the wetland and blanket bog deposits on Exmoor which is being planned at present. Though some analysis has been done in various areas of the uplands (e.g. Merryfield and Moore 1974) no work has been done in the coastal zone and, in order to establish the environmental context for past human activity, it is essential to develop a comprehensive programme of sampling, analysis and dating. Work in the coastal deposits should also enable connections to be made with processes and activity at other sites in the Severn Estuary and Bristol Channel.

The proximity and visibility of the Welsh Coast and islands in the Bristol Channel have resulted in plentiful trade and transportation by sea from the North Devon and Somerset Coasts which continued into the present century. As yet there is no direct evidence for prehistoric watercraft from the Exmoor coast, but since the discovery of the Ferriby boats in the late 1930s, the size and complexity of construction of early boats has been apparent (Wright 1990). The recent discovery at Dover has emphasised that they were not merely estuarine craft (Corfield 1993). Lost vessels and cargoes have been plentiful off this difficult coast, and though wary of the trap of pure speculation, it is likely that early craft plied the coast and it is possible that they ventured across the sea to Wales. In recent years fishermen in small boats out of Porlock have found themselves making unscheduled, but safe, crossings to South Wales (D. Partridge, *pers. comm*).

Dunster Marshes, further east along the coast, represent the final stage of silting-up in the valley of the River Avill during the 16th century, when the quay at Dunster was rendered inoperable (Binding and Stevens 1977, 50-51). There is undoubtedly great potential for investigation of the deposits at Dunster to determine whether they could preserve remains of the quay and the watercraft which used it. Such evidence would be fundamental to a better understanding of the nature of the medieval shipping in the Bristol Channel.

The plentiful food resources of the sea would have been invaluable to all generations of coastal communities on the Exmoor coast, whether fishing offshore, netting or trapping on the foreshore. 'V'-shaped rubble fish traps at Porlock Weir, Lynmouth and Minehead testify to the exploitation of fish and tide. Fishing has a long history as an industry out of small ports such as Lynmouth, where it dates back at least to the Medieval period, and traces of the herring fishing and processing survive there today, though the shoals departed in the mid-18th century (Mold 1992, 17). Proper investigation of existing and former ports, the foreshore and beaches may well yield more surviving evidence.

Long distance visibility from the cliffs was clearly the reason for the siting of two Roman fortlets on the coast at Old Burrow, Countisbury and Martinhoe, both in Devon. These two sites both dating to the mid-1st century AD., are among the few on Exmoor to have been excavated and published (Fox and Ravenhill 1966). The fortlets are of similar construction. Old Burrow was constructed first, *c*. 50-55 AD (pl.13.2) and superseded by Martinhoe which was occupied until about 70 AD. Their purpose was to watch over the Bristol Channel and in particular to raise the alarm if the Silures of South Wales attacked. With clear views to the Gower and Lavernock Point, east of Barry, as well as along the Devon and Somerset coasts, the fortlets were ideally placed to warn Roman ships patrolling in the Bristol Channel. The abandonment of Martinhoe coincides with the departure of the Second Augustan Legion from Exeter to Caerleon after the Silures had been subdued.

These two fortlets are thought to have been supplied by sea possibly from landing places at Glenthorne for Old Burrow and Heddon's Mouth or Woody Bay for Martinhoe (*ibid*). The Roman patrol in the Bristol Channel, probably from a fleet based at Sea Mills (Avonmouth) and the ferrying of supplies and men to garrison the fortlets would have created considerable maritime activity for nearly two decades; it is possible that more evidence, in the form of artefacts, installations or wrecks remains to be discovered in the vicinity.

Supply and transportation by sea were vital not only to the coastal communities but also to those who lived and worked further inland, where raising sheep and wood production dominated the economy from the medieval period onwards. Land communications were difficult and treacherous where they existed and largely non-existent for wheeled traffic until the 19th century. Pack ponies and sledges had been used to carry goods and the roads, even between significant places such as Lynton and South Molton, were no more than tracks over arduous territory (Mold 1992, 31). The provision of supplies not available locally and the export of local goods and products must have relied considerably on transport by sea, unless the 'products' could walk to market on their own hooves. Even the advent of the railways did not solve the problem because of the difficult terrain and resultant distance to railheads. In the age of motor vehicles the lack of road transport and consequent volume of sea traffic along a coast now more notable for tourism than trade, is not easy to imagine, but an example of the indispensability of maritime transport from the nineteenth century illustrates the point.

The coastal woodlands, farms and settlements created an integrated economy of timber production, oak coppice grown for tan bark and charcoal burning, agricultural production and fishing. Until the Second World War both Porlock and Lynmouth were busy small ports. In the mid-nineteenth century Porlock Weir harbour was the setting not only for boat building, for example, the smack 'John and William' was launched there in 1858 (Bouquet 1959, 142), but also for importing and exporting. The shipping enterprises of the Ridler family are well-documented by Bouquet (*op.cit*) and demonstrate a trading system in which oak bark was taken from Culbone Woods, and shipped from Porlock (with ballast from Porlock Weir brickworks, also owned by Ridler) and Lynmouth (where Ridler also had a bark yard) to Penzance; tin was shipped back from Penzance to South Wales, where it was replaced with a cargo of coal and limestone, which was shipped back to Porlock and Lynmouth. Cattle and sheep were taken from Porlock to South Wales, bricks and timber from Porlock to Bristol. A little further along the coast timber and pit-props were taken from Embelle Wood beach to South Wales, coal and limestone brought back to Glenthorne Beach to supply the mansion with fuel and the estate with lime to sweeten the fields. Lime kilns were built at the foot of the cliffs, near beaches which could be landed upon and in ports and havens; many examples survive, as at Heddon's Mouth, Lynmouth, Glenthorne and Bossington.

This example of nineteenth century entrepreneurial endeavour illustrates not only the importance of the ports and landings for both exportation and importation, but also the integration of different aspects of economic exploitation of the coastal zone and the sea. The combination of historical records and the archaeological evidence will provide a fuller picture than either can alone.

This consideration of Exmoor's maritime potential has ranged the length of its coast and has taken examples from post-glacial times to the twentieth century, there are many other aspects of its history which have left their mark in the landscape. The effects and residues of tourism, which began to develop at the time of the Napoleonic Wars, when the spectacular scenery of the coast substituted for the continent as a place for walking and Romantic inspiration are plentiful. The coast was also the focus for several country estates, the Hallidays at Glenthorne, the Newnes at Hollerday Hill, Lynton, the Littons at Ashley Combe, Porlock. Their fine houses, estate architecture and economic impact have all left their stamp. The defensive outposts of the Roman Empire have their successors in extensive Second World War military installations on the coast at North Hill and numerous pill boxes on the coast and shore.

From mesolithic hunter to twentieth century shipping company, man has exploited Exmoor's coastal resources. It falls to archaeologists to investigate and interpret this varied legacy and to seek to fulfil its maximum potential. Since 1991 some progress has been made in establishing archaeological priorities and taking action. In 1992 a major survey of the archaeology of Exmoor was begun by the RCHME and already the surveyors have recorded new sites in the coastal zone; their six-year programme will undoubtedly produce more evidence for coastal activities. The first stages of recording the submerged forest deposits at Porlock Weir completed in 1991 are intended to be only the first step towards better data and understanding of the coastal wetland. A survey of coastal military sites by the Fortress Study Group is beginning as this paper is written and the Exmoor Mines Research Group is starting to co-ordinate research and fieldwork on the extensive industrial sites, including coastal mining sites around Combe Martin. In 1992 the RCHME produced the first full survey of a class of monument on Exmoor, the lithic monuments (Quinnell and Dunn 1992). These beginnings will provide the information to guide archaeological policies in the National Park towards the best means of understanding, protecting and interpreting Exmoor's archaeology

and will establish the maritime element as a significant part of a coherent picture of the whole.

The mixture of prehistory, foreshore mud and industry will be one familiar to Ted Wright and to those who have also wrestled with the clays of North Ferriby. It is to be hoped that half a century after the finding of the North Ferriby Boats, those of us with the task of first exposing the fragments of the past of Exmoor and then reassembling them, will prove as assiduous and tenacious in completing it as Ted Wright has been with Ferriby.

## References

Aston, M. and Burrow, I. 1982. *The Archaeology of Somerset*. Taunton : Somerset County Council.

Binding, H. and Stevens, D. 1977. *Minehead - A New History*. Dulverton : Exmoor Press.

Bouquet, M. 1959. *No Gallant Ship*. London : Hollis and Carter.

Boyd Dawkins, W. 1870. On the discovery of flint and chert under a submerged forest in West Somerset. *Journal of the Ethnological Society*, New Series, Vol. II, 141-144.

Corfield, M. 1993. The First Cross-Channel Ferry? *English Heritage Conservation Bulletin* 19, 8-9.

Court, G. 1987. *Exmoor National Park*. Exeter : Webb and Bower.

Curtis, L.F. 1971. *Soils of Exmoor Forest*. Harpenden : Soil Survey Special Survey No. 5

Fox, A. and Ravenhill, W.L.D. 1966. Early Roman outposts on the North Devon Coast, Old Burrow and Martinhoe. *Proceedings of the Devon Archaeological Society* 24, 3-39.

Merryfield, D.L. and Moore, P.D. 1974. Prehistoric human activity and blanket peat initiation on Exmoor. *Nature* 250, 439-441.

Mold, E. 1992. *Lynton and her coast*. Barnstaple : Green Apple.

Quinnell, N.V. and Dunn, C.J. 1992. *Lithic monuments within the Exmoor National Park*. Royal Commission on Historical Monuments of England, unpublished report.

Wright, E.V. 1990. *The Ferriby Boats. Seacraft of the Bronze Age*. London : Routledge.

# 14

# THE MUSEUM DISPLAY OF EARLY BOATFINDS

## *Gillian Hutchinson*

It is a sad fact that the number of people who know about and are interested in early boats is very small. Members of the Prehistoric Society, the Nautical Archaeology Society and print-runs of specialist books on this topic can be numbered in hundreds rather than thousands. Archaeologists excavate early boats and museums preserve them because we specialists know that they are of great cultural significance. Our problem or challenge is how to inform and enthuse a wider audience.

Museums provide a great opportunity for putting a steady stream of thousands of people face-to-face with real objects. However, mere exposure to the objects does not guarantee "catching the bug", even though ancient wood may look as though it died of something contagious. There are still too many logboats festering in museum galleries, bereft of interpretation. This is the result of a curator-centric approach; "we have it, we think it is interesting so we will put it on display".

Visitors to a museum are conscious that there is more to see round the next corner. This may induce a feeling that they need to ration their attention and only apply their full concentration to an object if they are certain that the reward will justify the effort. It is rare for a museum visitor to spend more than a minute looking at any one exhibit and the attention span decreases the longer the visitor stays in the museum. The challenge, therefore, is to arrest the visitors' attention in the first place and then to convey with great immediacy, before they can slip away, what it is that we want them to perceive and remember about early boats.

Visitors are of course not an homogenous group. They are of all different ages and cognitive abilities, with varying degrees of prior knowledge and interest. They also behave differently depending on whether they are alone or with friends, family or school groups (McManus 1987). Na-

tional Maritime Museum visitor surveys show that only 10 to 15% of our visitors come unaccompanied. However some basic psychological principles about information receptivity are of general application.

A serious mistake on the part of museum curators is to think that the visitor's initial reaction to a display is intellectual. It is essentially impressionistic and can be influenced by the environment of the display almost as much as by the content. A good museum display can give a powerful sense of exploring the possibilities of experience beyond one's own day-to-day life. The effect of unintentional background sensations such as noise, smells, temperature and light levels may make the visitor less disposed to assimilating information. The ideal is to create an intriguing and unique sense of place through the associative implications of the material on display and its context. Props can be used to evoke the world beyond the museum and at another time. The technique adopted for the archaeology gallery at the National Maritime Museum involves re-creating the scenes of the excavations of boat-finds. This does not provide an illusion of transporting the visitor to these places, as is the intention with "experiences" such as Jorvik. At Greenwich the visitors stand outside the scenes, looking on across barriers surmounted by explanatory labels.

I have already suggested that the surviving remains of early boats can be aesthetically unappealing or even repellent. This may be particularly true in the context of a museum which contains high quality art objects, though conversely or perversely the contrast may help to grab the visitor's attention. It is a prime purpose of museums to display real artefacts and the visitor has a right to feel short-changed if presented with some kind of copy instead. This is not merely because of the quasi-magical property of objects to connect the present to past events and people, as with for example the "speaking trumpet used by Nelson at the Battle of Trafalgar". More fundamentally it is about allowing the visitor the opportunity to observe artefacts at first hand. However, in cases where so much deterioration has taken place since the artefact was excavated that it is no longer comprehensible to most visitors, substituting a replica of the artefact can be justified.

A factor other than aesthetic attractiveness which excites curiosity is the quality of being out of the ordinary. Prehistoric boats have an advantage in terms of large size, strange material and oddity of construction. Movement is eye-catching, so that it can be helpful to introduce dynamic processes and avoid static displays.

After the initial attraction a further set of factors determine whether the display will hold the visitor's attention. If it relates to what he or she already knows, and if the visitor realises that it can fill a previously unsuspected gap in his or her cognitive framework, the paths of communication are opened up. Relevance is of key importance. There was for example a notable increase in interest in the Ferriby boats as a result of the discovery of the Dover boat. If visitors have little or no prior knowledge of the subject matter their interest is far more likely to be sparked if they can relate to it on a personal and subjective, rather than an abstract and objective, level. People will be interested in something if it is of relevance to themselves, for example if an ancestor served on a ship featured in a display. With early boatfinds there is limited scope for exploiting this. People who live near where a boat was discovered may take some personal interest in it. People develop a personal interest in finding out more about the things they own and so the sale in the museum shop of a model kit of a boat on display would intensify interest in the original. People are also interested in stories, preferably with strong human interest, and want to find out what happened next. The excavation of boats often provides good material for this, with the classic plot of threat and rescue. Narrative can be difficult to follow when presented as static pictures and text and is more suited to video or film. The signals that visitors pick up cannot be accurately predicted. The retrieval of boat remains has always been an inelegant process and images of excavators going about their business may be alienating rather than attractive.

Turning now to the messages which the display is intended to communicate, the first thing we need to convey is an appreciation of how long ago the boats were built and used. The low-tech way of doing this is with a time-chart on the wall. The Jorvik centre uses a far more elaborate and space-consuming approach, transporting people in "time cars" through the intervening centuries to the Viking period. This may be effective but there is a risk that the visitor's thoughts will be distracted from the point of it all to the details of the tableaux. It would be desirable to establish a period context for the objects so that the visitor can relate them to how people lived at the time. Unfortunately not many people can conjure up clear mental images of the Bronze or Iron Ages. For more recent times a sense of period can be evoked by the use of contemporary

music. This cannot be done authentically for the distant past so modern compositions, which always seem to hint at dark skulduggery, are perhaps best avoided.

The second appreciation which we wish to convey is that of the technology. We want people to recognise that the Ferriby boats, for example, are very odd and that of the possible ways of building a boat this is not the most obvious. Building them was a remarkable technological achievement since the trees required were very large, the tools available were very limited and the shaping, jointing and fastening is of astonishing complexity. Writing statements to this effect on the wall is not an effective way of putting the message across. Only if people perceive these things for themselves will they become part of their mental furniture.

Learning in a museum environment is not simply a passive process of absorbing information from text panels and looking at the objects to which they refer. The acquisition of information from objects is an active, analytical task. Ideally we want the visitor to be sufficiently engaged by the objects to ask him or herself questions about them beyond the basic "what is that?" and "what's next?". Visitors can be prompted to do this by posing questions in the text of the display. Fact-finding sheets for schoolchildren can be used as a more structured aid for achieving this.

A certain amount of text is essential for making the links between objects and the subject-matter of the display. The purpose of the text is to make the display accessible to the visitor (Kentley and Negus 1989, 2). The most comprehensive reading is carried out by lone visitors and couples. Adult males, alone, in pairs or in small groups are most likely to read the text but they characteristically pay little attention to the objects being described. By contrast children tend to approach exhibits at a physical level and do not read text or observe graphics (McManus 1987, 266-8). Text of twenty words or less can be read in a five-second glance and is more likely to be taken in than long panels. Most visitors do not bother to read the instructions on interactive exhibits before they begin to manipulate them. They attempt to work out what they are about for themselves and only read directions or look at graphics as a last resort (McManus 1987, 266). There are opportunities for incorporating such "discovery learning" into displays about ancient boats, allowing visitors to handle exhibits rather than just to view them. For example, twisting and testing the strength of withies might be feasible within Health and Safety constraints, whereas practical experiment with replica tools might not.

The antithesis of discovery learning is the passive watching of a video. Videos can however make an important contribution to overall display strategy. Firstly, especially if the audience is seated to watch them, they detain visitors at a particular exhibit for considerably longer than would otherwise be the case. The use of the human voice rather than print makes verbal information easier to absorb and moving pictures can show activities, such as excavation and boatbuilding techniques, which are beyond the capabilities of static display. One way of conveying information about the technology of early boatbuilding would be to show the film of a replica-building project, including the felling of trees, the cutting and fastening of the boat components and the boat in use. There is a danger of creating false impressions, since we do not know exactly how any of these processes were carried out, and a further danger of removing the sense of mystery if it appears that we know all that there is to know. The ideal is to inform and stimulate the imagination, not to satiate it. Computer graphics which show how the timber for the components was converted from tree trunks could be effective, although impersonal. Both computer graphics and three-dimensional models have the draw-back that they do not convey just how big the actual artefacts are or were. The ideal gallery would have sufficient space to show the full extent not only of the recovered part of the boat but also its reconstructed original dimensions, as well as sufficient height to be able to represent the dimensions of one of the parent trees.

Ted Wright is fond of saying that what we need is "fire in the belly". There is a risk that long familiarity with ancient boatfinds can make us not so much ablaze as blasé, and consequently less able to communicate enthusiasm for the subject to others. I was taken aback, when first seeing the new Bronze Age boat being excavated at Dover, to feel quite overwhelmed by elation. Somehow we need to design our displays to convey more than factual information about the early boats which have been found, to share with the visitors our pride of possession.

## References

Kentley, E. and Negus, D. 1989. *Writing on the Wall. A Guide for Presenting Exhibition Text.* Greenwich: National Maritime Museum.

McManus, P. M. 1987. It's the company you keep... The social determination of learning-related behaviour in a science museum. *Int. J. Museum Management and Curatorship* 6, 263-270.

Schouten, F. 1987. Psychology and exhibit design: a note. *Int. J. Museum Management and Curatorship* 6, 259-262.

# SEWN BOATS OF THE INDIAN OCEAN: A COMMON TRADITION?

## *Eric Kentley*

In *A Handbook of Sewn Boats*, Professor Prins attempts to synthesise a vast amount of material from archaeologists, ethnographers, travellers and his own research in the field and in museums around the world. Assembling details across time and space, from the Ferriby to the islands of Oceania, he arrives at a typology of sewn boats (that is, boats on which the planking is fastened not by metal but some form of fibre rope). He modestly describes the work as 'merely one particular mode of ordering the data...'(Prins 1984, 11).

Such a wide-ranging survey inevitably gives only a brief summary of many sewn boat types; filling in the details, where they can still be found, is left to future researchers. In this paper I will add a little to the account of some sewn boats of the Indian Ocean, and in doing so attempt to demonstrate that it is not a coincidence of typology that puts most of the Indian Ocean boats into one category, but a common, unique feature.

Around the Indian Ocean, Prins finds the dominant method of sewing a plank boat to be the continuous sewing of edge-to-edge planking using plugs to stop up the sewing holes with dowels between the planks - his permutation P9 out of a total of sixteen possibilities. This permutation is almost unique to the Indian Ocean, from East Africa to the East Coast of India. The only P9 boat recorded outside this area is the Ljubljana boat. P9 would therefore seem to be the Indian Ocean tradition. However, P9 may not be the only permutation found within the area. Prins suggests that there may also be the permutations P10, which is the same as P9 but without dowels - for example the masula of India's east coast and the Chittagong *balam*; and P12, the same as P9 but without dowels or plugs - to which he classifies the *oruwa* of Sri Lanka.

In 1983/84, largely as a consequence of Ted Wright's interest in possible ethnographic comparisons with the

sewing on the Ferriby boats, I was able to make a study of the masula surf boat. This is a European term for the sewn plank boat found (although not continuously) from Paradeep in Orissa to Karaikal, south of Madras, in Tamil Nadu (Kentley 1985). Historically, such boats were used to carry cargo and passengers between the shore and ships anchored in the open roadsteads. With the development of artificial harbours along the coast, boats are no longer needed for such work, and all sewn boats are now fishing craft. With a few exceptions, they are used for beach seining. Prins is essentially correct in his classification. All use continuous sewing between edge-to-edge planking and none have dowels between the planks. The holes bored through the planks for the sewing rope are plugged either with wooden pegs (in the south) or with balls of coconut fibre (in the north).

It is the lack of dowels between the planks that, according to Prins's classification, puts the masula out of the mainstream of the Indian Ocean sewn boat tradition. Similarly, the *oruwa* of Sri Lanka is isolated by having neither dowels or plugs. But the *oruwa* is not a plank boat: it is a logboat with a sewn-on washstrake. The washstrake is well above the waterline - there is no need for plugging. Indeed the sewn plank boat of the island, the flat-bottomed *paruwa* (plural *paru*) has its sewing holes plugged below the waterline, but not above. Exactly the same practice is found on the masula - above the waterline the holes are left unplugged. Thus, however we classify the masula and *paruwa* we must also classify the *oruwa*. Plugged holes are not a defining trait.

But even ignoring the plugs, these three craft are, in Prins's terms, still isolated from all other Indian Ocean sewn boats by having no dowels between the planks. There is no evidence of the masula or *paruwa* ever having been built with dowels. Indeed the builders of masula say that the boat is built so that the plank edges can, to some extent,

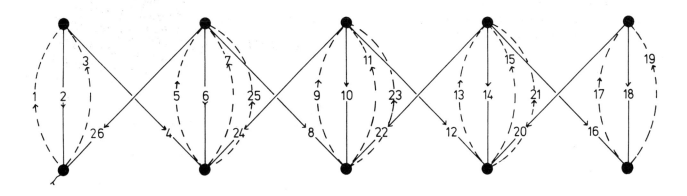

*Fig. 15.1 The standard Indian Ocean sewing method*

slide against each other as the boat rides through the heavy surf. Dowels would prevent this. (Whether this has any real advantage in allowing the planks a limited freedom of movement is debatable: a few metal-fastened beach seining boats operate on the coast, apparently successfully.) But is the absence of dowels sufficiently important to justify the separate classification of these boats from the other sewn boats of the Indian Ocean?

The masula and *paruwa* are certainly distinct from other Indian Ocean sewn boats by having no frames (although the *paruwa* has floors crossing the boat's bottom) - the sides being held apart by cross-beams. I believe they are the only flat-bottomed sewn boats of the area. The masula and *paruwa* are also very different from each other, despite both being beach seiners. Masulas are fine-sterned, *paru* are scow-ended at both bow and stern. Not all *paru* are the same - a few are narrow with an outrigger, most are not. Masulas also vary considerably in design, from the truly flat-bottomed and crudely built boats of Orissa to the more rounded, expertly constructed boats of Andhra Pradesh.

However, by concentrating on dissimilarities and the absence of dowels, we are overlooking what these boats have in common with the other Indian Ocean craft - the actual pattern of sewing. The quickest flick through *A Handbook of Sewn Boats* make clear the enormous variety of sewing patterns on boats around the world, yet from Mombasa to Madras, on the *mtepe*, the *beden* of Somalia (Chittick 1980) and *sanbuq* of Oman (Facey 1979), the dhow built for Tim Severin by Laccadive Islanders (Severin 1982), the boats of Kerala, the *oruwa*, *paruwa* and masula, the pattern of sewing seems to be identical. Paris (1841) illustrates a number of sewn boats of the Indian Ocean - the masula, *paruwa*, Muscat *béden*, Sri Lankan *yathra dhoni* and boats of Managlore - all of which appear to have sewing consistent with today's pattern.

Holes are bored right through the planking. From outboard the sewing looks discontinuous, simply three (or six if the rope is doubled) loops running through each separate pair of holes. Inboard, the pairs of holes are again connected by a loop but there is also a criss-cross of rope

joining adjacent pairs of sewing holes (fig.15.1). The sewing pattern is often reversed - i.e. the criss-cross pattern is outboard - where the stem and sternposts are joined to the plank ends (pl.15.1). This criss-cross pattern forms a web to hold some form of wadding material (often coir fibre) in position along the seam of the two planks (fig.15.2). On contact with water the wadding material expands, thus tightening the sewing and pulling the planks closer together.

Theoretically, there are several ways of producing this pattern of a web on one side of the hull. On the East Coast of India and in Sri Lanka, at least, there is only one way. Sewing commences amidships and runs towards the bow or stern, producing a series of linked 'N' patterns inboard. On reaching the end, the sewing returns to its starting point. Prins (1984, 87) also records this method as used on *mtepe* models. I have seen no evidence for another method. However, Prins records a method which produces the criss-cross pattern on one side of the hull and a series of 'N's on the other. It also differs from the Indian/Sri Lankan method by making three runs - finishing at the furthest point, not at the starting point. This could be advantageous on a vessel as large as a *mtepe*. But it is a method used by model makers - there is no evidence of it on an actual boat. It is, on the other hand, quite common to see 'N's on one side of the hull and separate loops on the other, particularly around the gunwale - this is simply a 'half sewn' seam.

This 'Indian Ocean' method appears to stop on the coast of East Africa. According to Prins (1984, 158-9), it does not travel inland, the canoes of Lake Victoria being lashed together, not truly sewn. The easternmost representative of the method may be the Chittagong *balam*. Greenhill (1971, 113) states:

*The seam between plank and dugout is ... caulked with teased-out old rope and the whole packed on both sides with a seal of grey mud. Over this mud strips of the broad green leaves of palms are laid, and over these in turn tightly bunched long coarse grasses. On the outside of the boat the whole seam is finished off with a protective cover of split bamboo strips... [P]lank and dugout [are] held together with a tight sewing of split bamboo, the stitch crossed diagonally between the paired holes inside the boat but not on the outside.*

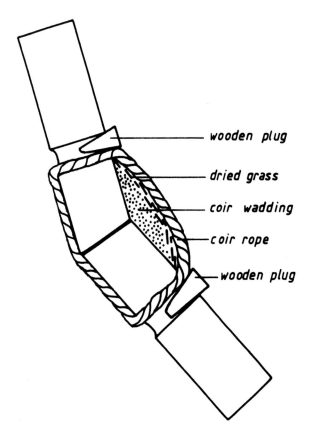

*Fig. 15.2 Cross-section of Tamil Nadu masula sewing*

A photograph of the inboard of a *balam* under construction published in a later work (Greenhill 1976, 136) shows the sewing pattern, from this view at least, to be identical to the standard Indian Ocean criss-cross pattern. However, it is not standard practice to give the seam a protective cover outboard, held in place by the sewing loops, although this is seen on some masulas where the

plank edges are particularly worn. Bamboo is not the usual sewing material around the Indian Ocean - coir rope is traditional, although synthetic materials are becoming common. Again, coir fibre is the usual wadding material, not grasses, although this practice is also followed by the Orissa masula builders.

But if the *balam* is not the easternmost example of the 'pure Indian Ocean' method, is the masula? The answer is complicated. The masulas of Tamil Nadu do indeed show the typical web pattern on the inside of the hull and separate loop pattern outboard. However, where the plank ends are joined to the posts, the pattern is not simply reversed as is usual on other Indian Ocean boats - a slightly different method of sewing is used. This produces a web - the standard criss-cross with loops - on *both* sides of the hull (fig.15.3 and pl.15.2). The advantage is that it allows wadding material to be held on both sides of the seams, presumably making a tighter joint. Further north along the coast, separated by the deltas of the Krishna and Godavari rivers, this method is used on *all* seams, not just at the posts, on the sewn boats of Andhra Pradesh and Orissa.

It is, of course, impossible to trace the origin of this variation. It may simply be a local development to cope with the exceptionally high surf on this coast, giving extra strength to the plank joins. There is no firm evidence that the double web method has ever been more widespread than it is today. Of the numerous illustrations of Madras masulas made from the 17th century onwards, none show clearly the use of the double web here on plank-to-plank seams. Early illustrations may indicate webbing outboard - for example a 17th-century sketch by Thomas Bowrey (Hill 1958, 215) - but this could be explained by Paris's (1841, plate 27) plan of a masula which shows the webbing outboard on all the side planking, with the separate loops inboard, with the reverse on the bottom planking seams. No double web is shown on the post/plank seams.

Paris illustrates the same arrangement on the *paruwa* (his plate 24), which is still built in this way. The masula is not. A mid-19th century model in the National Maritime

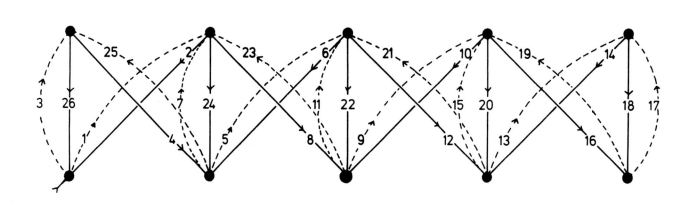

*Fig. 15.3 Northern masula 'double web sewing'*

Museum shows the patterns that are still found on the masulas around Madras today: webbing on the inside only on strake-to-strake seams; a double web at the post/plank seams.

The double web is not seen in Sri Lanka. The *oruwa* and *paruwa* conform completely to the standard Indian Ocean method. Prins's East African *mtepe* model variation, mentioned above, neither follows the steps of the masula sewing nor gives the same result, although it does produce a web both inboard and outboard. The double web of the masula seems to be unique.

The steps involved in producing this pattern are different to those that produce the standard Indian Ocean pattern. The Chittagong *balam*, at the extreme end of the distribution of sewn boats in the Indian Ocean, also seems exceptional, in having, in addition to a web inboard, a protective strip outboard held simply between the loops of stitching. Should these craft be considered as outside the Indian Ocean tradition?

It is by examining the extremes, the exceptions, and comparing examples from outside the area that the essential characteristics are revealed. I have argued above that dowels and plugs are simply refinements - not defining traits. If we look at the sewn boats further east, for example in Viet Nam (Manguin 1985, 321-7), again we find the sewing holding a form of wadding or a batten in place. One striking difference is that the sewing holes are not bored straight through the planks but are angled. However, further east on the Manilla *casco* and Hainan fishing boat they are bored straight through (Manguin 1985, 326). So holes drilled straight through the planks are a characteristic but not exclusive feature of Indian Ocean boats. More importantly, on these South-East Asian boats the sewing is discontinuous - each pair of holes is sewn separately. These loops are deemed sufficient to hold wadding or battens in position. Again, wadding is a characteristic but not exclusive feature of the Indian Ocean boats. What now stands out as the single exclusive feature is the criss-cross web that holds the wadding material.

If this is taken as the defining feature the *balam*, irrespective of its outboard seam covering, and the of Andhra Pradesh and Orissa, with their double webs, are all within the Indian Ocean tradition.

It is remarkable that there appears to be no evidence of a simplification of the web within the area. For example, Prins (1984, 101) publishes a photograph of the web on an *oruwa* where a batten is used instead of fibre wadding. In theory, the batten could be held in place by a much simpler sewing method - a continuous loop for example. But perhaps there is evidence. Bidault (1945, 273) provides details of another group of sewn boats with fibrous wadding but which is held in position not by a web but by a continuous zig-zag pattern. These craft are found in Chad. Is this a completely different, separately developed technique, or a simplification of the Indian Ocean technique? Only further research can shed light.

# References

Bidault, J. 1945. *Pirogues et Pagaies*. Paris: J Susse.

Chittick, N. 1980. Sewn boats in the Western Indian Ocean and a survival in Somalia. *Int. J. Naut. Archaeol.* 9, 297-309.

Facey, W. 1979. *Oman: a seafaring nation*. Muscat: Ministry of Information and Culture.

Greenhill, B. 1971. *Boats and boatmen of Pakistan*. Newton Abbot: David & Charles.

Greenhill, B. 1976. *Archaeology of the boat*. London: Adam & Charles Black.

Hill, A.H. 1958. Some accounts of the Oriental boat. *Mariner's Mirror* 44, 201-17.

Kentley, E. 1985. Some aspects of the masula surf boat. In S. McGrail & E. Kentley (eds.) *Sewn plank boats*. Greenwich: BAR International Series 276, 303-17.

Manguin, P-Y. 1985. Sewn-plank craft of South-East Asia. In S. McGrail & E. Kentley (eds.) *Sewn plank boats*. Greenwich: BAR International Series 276, 319-43.

Paris, F.E. 1841. *Essai sur la construction navale des peuples extra-européens...* Paris: Arthus Bertrand.

Prins, A.H.J. 1986. *A handbook of sewn boats*. London: National Maritime Museum Monographs & Reports 59.

Severin, T. 1982. *The Sindbad voyage*. London: Hutchinson.

# 16

# TALES FROM THE RIVERBANK:
## Bronze Age palaeochannels in the alluviated Nedern Valley at Caldicot Castle Lake, Gwent

### *Nigel Nayling*

In May 1988, during the construction of a lake in the grounds of the Caldicot Castle Country Park, Gwent (ST 4880 8860), waterlogged timbers were observed and work halted to allow for archaeological investigations. Brief excavations in 1988 and 1989 indicated the presence of a silted palaeochannel of the River Nedern, a minor tributary of the Severn, containing well preserved spreads of wood, stone and artefactual material including a Wilburton style chape (Parry 1989; Parry and Parkhouse 1990). The uncertain long-term survival of organics within the disturbed deposits generated discussions between the local authorities, Cadw and the Glamorgan-Gwent Archaeological Trust which led to funding for a programme of three years of excavation and two years of post-excavation leading to publication.

The exposed deposits were situated in the river valley bottom just to the east of the present course of the Nedern, at a point where the valley narrows with a spur of hard geology to the west (on which the medieval Caldicot Castle was constructed) and outcrops of Carboniferous strata to the east (pl.16.1). To the south, the present river flows out onto the Caldicot Levels before entering the Severn Estuary.

## Objectives and Strategy

The research design developed as the project progressed, with aims and objectives being assessed prior to commencement of each of the three seasons of excavation, reflecting an increasing appreciation of the complexity of the surviving deposits. The primary aims were to selectively excavate the palaeochannel features exposed, to elucidate the sequence of aggradation and erosion events preserved within these, excavate structures and associated artefactual material and relate them to this sequence, and execute a sampling strategy to clarify contemporary environment while maintaining safe working conditions. The near neutral pH of the deposits was evident from the excellent survival of the faunal remains recovered. This suggested that, in addition to acceptable survival of pollen and macroscopic plant material, calcareous environmental indicators such as diatoms, ostracods, mollusca and coleoptera should be well preserved. Hence, a multi-disciplinary environmental programme formed an integral part of the project from the outset. Initially, excavation strategy (Harris 1989, 15-18) concentrated on an 'open area' approach, to optimise appreciation of the distribution of material within the palaeochannel. However, both changes in project personnel, and difficulties in identifying the stratigraphic sequence led to a trend towards increasing use of linear trenches oriented at right angles to the predominant palaeochannel axis. This allowed for more detailed recording of the stratigraphy with sections giving continuous confirmation of the sequence. The move towards increasing use of stratigraphic rather than arbitrary excavation processes (Harris 1989,18-21), has given justifiable rewards in terms of closer understanding of the succession of scouring and silting events with which the artefactual material was associated.

## Methodology and Logistics

Machining had created a kidney-shaped hole approximately 65m long, 30m wide and 2.5m deep with sloping sides cutting through modern to prehistoric alluvium which in wet weather collected water and became dangerously slippery, and in dry conditions rapidly dessicated resulting in cracking and oxidation of the surface, threatening the integrity of the organic contents of the palaeochannel fills. Sensitive deposits were protected either by covering them with agricultural plastic or selectively flooding them using 2" and 6" pumps and dams for water management. Safe access necessitated the construction of scaffolding and plank ramps with a combination of scaffolding frameworks and adapted horticultural 'polytunnels' being placed over excavation areas to control both evaporation and the ingress of rainwater, and to provide suspended platforms from which staff could excavate deposits without standing on delicate wood spreads. However, these structures proved costly and time-consuming to build and maintain so that in the latter stages of the excavation, with a trend towards trenching, more extensive use was made of temporary planking straddling trench edges or small wooden pads placed on the excavation surface to give access, with lengths of agricultural plastic being employed to cover wood spreads to minimise evaporation.

Wood and deposits required frequent watering with mains-supplied hoses and hand-held sprays to reduce desiccation. Whilst rapid lifting of wood following *in situ* recording was preferred, when this was not possible (eg where timbers had been driven through earlier concentrations of wood debris), wood was sprayed and wrapped in 'clingfilm' and/or foam to maintain its water content and surface condition. Individual wood pieces were numbered with 'dymotape' labels attached with stainless steel mapping pins. After photography and drawing *in situ*, it proved most efficient for a wood specialist to lift, clean and record each piece on site using a standard wood record sheet (*cf* Coles 1990, 8-11). Samples were then taken for species identification, tree-ring counts and dendrochronology as appropriate. Pieces selected for further study (eg woodworking technology) and/or conservation were sheathed in nylon mesh and held in temporary storage tanks prior to transportation to a dedicated wood store in Caldicot Castle. Bone, ceramic and stone finds were individually numbered, bagged, cleaned and control air-dried on site.

## Interim Results

Selective excavation has resulted in the recovery of nearly 5000 wood items and in excess of 1000 bone fragments concentrated in the basal fills of numerous channel cuts evident as erosive interfaces in the stratigraphic sequence. Radiocarbon determinations indicate a date range of some thousand radiocarbon years (*c*.2500-3500BP). For the purposes of description, this sequence has been grouped along the lines advocated by Needham (1992, 259-260) into 'alluvial parcels' distinctive in terms of date and sedimentary characteristics.

Limited excavation and augering have revealed a pre-channel sequence of horizontally bedded blue grey clays reminiscent of the Wentlooge formation observed in the intertidal zone of the Severn Estuary (Allen 1987, 161-163). Several clearly defined organic horizons (at *c*.2.5-2.7m OD) may reflect periods of relative stability in sea level and possible salt-marsh formation. Radiocarbon

determinations from sediment samples of 4360±80BP (CAR-1322) and 4670±80BP (CAR-1323) indicate a Neolithic date. At the edges of the modern lake, where truncation by machining has been less severe, pre-channel sediments survive up to a height of *c*.4.5m OD. No direct evidence of human activity was observed in this sequence.

The earliest channel identified ran approximately northwest to south-east, being characterised by silty relatively inorganic fills and a steep, straight side along the northeast edge. Due to the considerable depth of this channel (base at *c*.1.7m OD), and its early position in the stratigraphic sequence, this was only excavated to base at one location where a dump of stone containing a few fragments of bone and wood (giving a radiocarbon date of 3430±70BP [CAR-1415]) predated a pile structure comprising several lines of pointed hazel posts driven into the edge of the channel (radiocarbon 3620±70BP [CAR-1317] and 3550±70BP [CAR-1314]). Other elements included a small group of piles approximately 1m northeast of the main group, several worked but disturbed horizontal timbers, and a single very thick roundwood pile to the south-east. The presence of articulated skeletons of flatfish (possibly flounder) in the basal fills of the channel, and interim results of ostracod studies (E Robinson, *pers. comm.*) perhaps suggest this channel was estuarine.

The north-east edge of this channel had been truncated by a later group of channels distinctive for containing highly organic basal fills with dense concentrations of wood with occasional inclusions of stone and faunal material. Radiocarbon dates cluster in the range 3150-3450BP. The major item recovered was a large plank derived from a mature oak tree (pl.16.2) which has been interpreted as a probable side strake from a plank sewn boat in the Ferriby tradition (Parry and McGrail 1991). This appears to have been damaged in antiquity and given the absence of further substantial elements of such a vessel, its deposition probably reflects a repair episode rather than the abandonment of a complete boat. Dating by dendrochronology has proved unsuccessful but a sample of oak heartwood has given a high precision radiocarbon determination of 3430±19BP (UB-3472). Two twisted yew withies excavated nearby may be fragments of the original stitching material used to attach the plank to adjacent elements in the parent boat. The bulk of the wood assemblage however is made up of unconverted hazel roundwood with relatively small quantities of blackthorn, alder and willow/poplar also present. A small number of oak and ash radial woodchips suggest carpentry activities. A spread of yew 'withies' recovered in the east half of the modern lake bed, many split or with cut ends, could be the fragmented remnants of a basketry item. Three wood pieces (two of hazel and one of Pomoideae) showed clear gnaw marks of beaver. No *in situ* structures were identified in this phase.

The subsequent alluvial parcel, comprising finely laminated organic clays contained by one or more channel cuts located further north-east again, truncated much of the earlier wood rich channels' fills. A distinctive characteristic of this phase is very low concentrations of wood. The sparse artefactual material recovered could indeed be residual debris from earlier channel fills as it is located on the interface with these earlier sediments although a single radiocarbon date of 3000±60BP (CAR-1407) does suggest some temporal separation.

This parcel was in turn largely eroded by a complex of relatively inorganic clays contained within a succession of closely intercut erosive interfaces interpreted as the southwest slopes of a group of palaeochannels. Very little of this parcel survived later scouring events but some basal fills remained containing spreads of wood, stone and bone.

The most completely preserved parcel comprised a wide (c.6.5m), flat-bottomed channel running approximately north-west to south-east across the base of the modern lake. Radiocarbon determinations from immature roundwood cluster in the region 3000-2900BP. Its basal fills contained dense spreads of stone, wood and faunal remains. Given the relatively fine particle size of contemporary basal sediments, the stone appears to have been dumped deliberately. Signs of heat damage (J Horek, *pers. comm.*) suggest that much of this is waste from cooking activities, but more extensive study is required. The wood assemblage was dominated by hazel roundwood, a proportion of it showing signs of working with lesser amounts of Pomoideae, blackthorn and alder roundwood also present. A wide variety of structural timbers (fig.16.1) of oak, ash and hazel, including double and single mortised planks were recovered. One of these (332) has provided a winter felling date through dendrochronology of 998/997BC (J Hillam, *pers. comm.*). Some had been pegged down into the river-bed (pl.16.3), although these did not form any clear linear distribution which might suggest the remnants of a trackway. Driven piles, predominantly of oak, formed no clear pattern, although some of these may relate to somewhat later activity. The faunal material was dominated by domesticates with a surprisingly high proportion of sheep. Metrical data will be limited by the large quantity that had been broken to enable marrow extraction. Other domesticate species present included cattle, pig, horse and dog (F McCormick, *pers. comm.*). Wild species, some of clearly natural presence rather than the result of human deposition, included water vole, toad, mallard/widgeon, barn owl, little grebe, heron and crane. A single bone of beaver has been identified (S Hamilton-Dyer, *pers. comm.*). Three metalwork items, a Wilburton style chape, a diminutive stub chape and a small coil of decorated tin (P Northover, *pers. comm.*) are associated with this phase.

Following some silting of this channel with relatively inorganic clays, two structures were placed in the river. A possible bridge or jetty consisting of two parallel lines of posts, approximately 2m apart was constructed across the channel. It comprised substantial driven posts at intervals of approximately 2m along each line, with smaller roundwood hazel poles with sharpened ends infilling between (pl.16.4). Although the posts are predominantly unconverted oak with finely tooled points, some split oak had been used along with non-oak timbers including a massive radially split ash plank with a mortise. The latter has given a winter felling date of 990/989BC (J Hillam, *pers. comm.*). This double line continues to the north-east beyond the rescue area so its full extent is unclear. A linear spread of wood debris, discarded timber, fragmentary hurdle-work and stone slabs ran obliquely from the channel edge towards this structure. Given dendrochronology dates in the late 990s BC from ash wood chips within this spread, it could be interpreted as a trackway facilitating access to the centre of the channel during construction of the possible bridge.

In the east half of the modern lake, upper fills of this large channel produced little artefactual material with the exception of a near complete and partially articulated male dog skeleton. It was an aged specimen with arthritic joints, heavily worn teeth, a healed femoral fracture, a healed skull fracture and a further head wound which was the probable cause of death (F McCormick, *pers. comm.*).

The latest channel encountered was located in the east half of the lake only and contained a finely laminated sequence of alternately organic and inorganic silts and clays. Cultural material was concentrated in the basal organic sediments comprising numerous roundwood pieces many with cut ends, oak chips, bone and a collapsed split oak post with a faceted point and a tenon at its upper end. Artefacts included a poorly preserved alder trough, a ladle or scoop and several sherds of pottery with incised chevrons and horizontal lines. It proved possible to open a cutting into the slope of the modern lake at its southern edge. Although still partially truncated by machining, the eastern edge of this late palaeochannel survived up to 4.5m OD, a metre higher than in the base of the lake. The uppermost channel fills, sealed below oxidised estuarine (?) clays, comprised silty clays with increasing organic content with depth. Wood was scarce and poorly preserved but spreads of charcoal, occasional animal bone and a single amber bead were recovered. Two sloping features, partially collapsed tunnels within the river bank, may be the partial remains of animal burrows although they do not closely parallel modern examples of either otter or beaver activity.

## Conclusions

Ongoing sedimentary and environmental studies are likely to clarify the fluvial processes involved in site formation and the contemporary nature of the palaeochannels and their wider environmental setting. Interim data suggest the sequence represents fortuitous survival of debris generated by adjacent human activity within a succession of scouring and silting events reflecting natural river channel movement and sedimentation. Data on contemporary river regimes, in particular on flow rates, will have important implications for understanding the taphonomy of artefact distributions.

Analysis of the wood assemblage will provide insights into possible woodland management and exploitation,

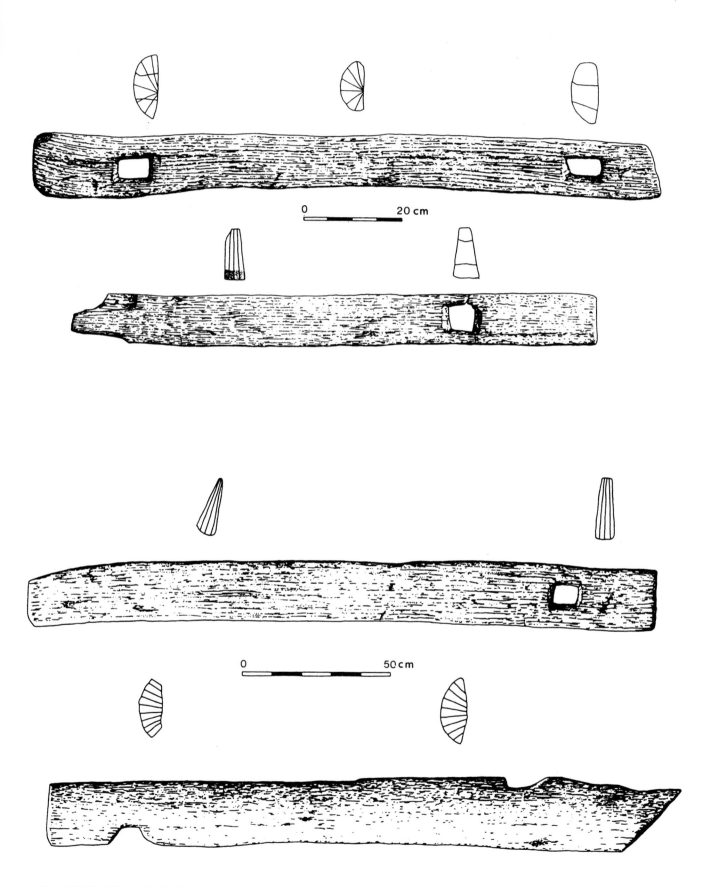

*Fig. 16.1 Caldicot Castle Lake: late Bronze Age worked timbers from the major palaeochannel.*

Nigel Nayling

species selection, craft activities and development of woodworking technology. The boat find is of particular interest given recent finds at Goldcliff (Bell 1992) and Dover (Bennett 1992) indicating a long-lived and wide-spread tradition of plank-sewn boats similar in many respects to the Ferriby vessels (Wright 1990). Although only 11 pieces of wood exhibited clear beaver chew marks, this species' potential for affecting landscapes and hydro-logical systems (Coles 1992) cannot be ignored. The considerable faunal collection, largely derived from the later phases in association with heat-damaged stone, implies adjacent food preparation based predominantly on domesticates but supplemented by wild species, particu-larly wildfowl.

Detailed comparison with broadly similar Bronze Age palaeochannel groups such as Wallingford (Lambrick 1992), Anslow's Cottages (Lobb 1992) and Runnymede Bridge (Needham 1991) should prove enlightening. In a regional context, the high level of archaeological activity within the Severn Levels, both in the development threat-ened Gwent Levels and in the intertidal zone of the Severn Estuary have and continue to generate data on contempo-rary sea level change, landscape development and settle-ment.

*Acknowledgements*. The project is jointly funded by Cadw (Welsh Historic Monuments), Monmouth Borough Coun-cil and Gwent County Council. My thanks to all those who formed part of the excavation team, which worked in uncomfortable and sometimes abysmal conditions, the numerous specialists involved for interim results and the staff of the Monmouth Museums Service for continuing assistance. The timber illustrations were drawn by Aidan O'Sullivan.

References

Allen, J.R.L. 1987. Late Flandrian shoreline oscillations in the Severn Estuary: the Rumney Formation at its typesite (Cardiff area). *Phil. Trans. R. Soc. Lond.* B315, 157-184.

Bell, M. 1992. Field Survey and Excavation at Goldcliff 1992. In M. Bell (ed), *Severn Estuary Levels Research Com-mittee Annual Report 1992*, 15-30. Aberystwyth: Cambrian Printers.

Bennett, P. 1992. The discovery and lifting of a middle Bronze Age boat at Dover. *Past* 14, 1-2. London: Prehistoric Society.

Coles, J.M. 1990. *Waterlogged wood: Guidelines on the recording, sampling, conservation, and curation of struc-tural wood.* London: English Heritage.

Coles, B. 1992. Further thoughts on the impact of beaver on temperate landscapes. In S. Needham and M.G. Macklin (eds), *Alluvial Archaeology in Britain*, 93-102. Oxbow Monograph 27.

Harris, E.C. 1989. *Principles of archaeological stratigra-phy*. 2nd edition. London: Academic Press

Lambrick, G. 1992. Alluvial archaeology of the Holocene in the Upper Thames Basin 1971-1991: a review. In S. Needham and M. Macklin (eds), *Alluvial Archaeology in Britain*, 209-228. Oxbow Monograph 27.

Lobb, S.J. 1992. Archaeological Investigations at Anslow's Cottages, Burghfield. In C.A. Butterworth and S.J. Lobb (eds), *Excavations in the Burghfield Area, Berkshire*, 79-169. Wessex Archaeology Report No.1. Salisbury: Trust for Wessex Archaeology Ltd.

Needham, S. 1991. *Excavation and Salvage at Runnymede Bridge, 1978: The Late Bronze Age Waterfront Site.* London: British Museum Press.

Needham, S. 1992. Holocene alluviation and interstratified settlement evidence in the Thames valley at Runnymede Bridge. In S. Needham and M.G. Macklin (eds), *Alluvial Archaeology in Britain*, 249-260. Oxbow Monograph 27, 1992.

Parry, S. J. 1989. Caldicot Castle Lake. In P. Crew (ed) *Archaeology in Wales* 28, 1988, 55-56. Porthmadog: Council for British Archaeology Group 2: Wales.

Parry, S. J. and Parkhouse, J. 1990. Caldicot Castle Lake. In P. Crew and S. Crew (eds) *Archaeology in Wales* 29, 1989, 47-48. Porthmadog: Council for British Archaeol-ogy Group 2: Wales.

Parry, S. and McGrail, S. 1991. A prehistoric boat fragment and a hard from Caldicot Castle Lake, Gwent, Wales. *Int. J. Naut. Archaeol.* 20.4:321-324.

Wright, E. 1990. *The Ferriby Boats. Seacraft of the Bronze Age.* London: Routledge.

# 17

# THE RESCUE OF DOVER'S BRONZE AGE BOAT

## *Keith Parfitt and Valerie Fenwick*

### *The Discovery* (KP)

As a Kentish land archaeologist, it was pure coincidence that I heard Mr Edward Wright give an interesting after-dinner speech at Bristol in 1991 concerning his discovery of the Bronze Age boats at North Ferriby. A year later, an unexpected find at Dover once again brought me into contact with the ever helpful Ted Wright. We contribute the following brief note on the discovery of Dover's Bronze Age boat in gratitude for all Ted's advice and assistance during the course of the boat's recovery.

In constructional details there are some remarkable similarities between the Dover boat and the Ferriby find of 1937, yet the location and discovery circumstances could hardly have been more dissimilar: half a century later and over 300 km to the south, the situation at Dover in 1992, on a deep building site within the heart of a busy working town, contrasted sharply with the desolate isolation of the Humber foreshore before the last war. However, these two sites, each with their own considerable difficulties of excavation, are now closely linked, both having produced vital remains of complex Bronze Age craft and both, to a greater or lesser degree, being associated with the name of Ted Wright.

The close proximity of Dover to the Continent and its location beside the River Dour within the only significant gap in many kilometres of chalk cliffs has ensured the settlement's standing as an important port for centuries. During 1991 the construction of a major new road, in the form of the A 20, posed a considerable threat to the buried archaeology within the maritime quarters of the old town (fig.17.1). Canterbury Archaeological Trust, funded by English Heritage, has been working on the project since June 1991 and much interesting information has been recorded.

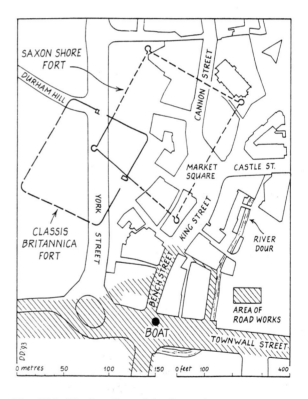

*Fig. 17.1 The location of the Dover boat*

At lunch-time on 28th September 1992 a team member spotted several timbers in the bottom of a deep contractor's pit dug for a new ground-water pumping station, at the junction of Bench Street and Townwall Street. The waterlogged timbers lay some 6m from pavement level, just below Ordnance Datum and a rapid inspection indicated that they formed part of a boat; moreover, the use of twisted withies in the construction, and the associated tufa and peat sediments suggested that the vessel was prehistoric. It became clear that the remains represented the substantially complete mid-section of a very well pre-served prehistoric sewn-plank boat, broadly similar to those found at North Ferriby.

Numerous telephone calls and meetings the following day culminated in the allocation of just six days to fully excavate and record the remains. Since the boat would have to be removed to allow the contractors to complete their work, it was decided that the remains must be lifted. The main problem to resolve was whether to attempt this in one, or to cut the boat into sections and lift these individually. Eventually it was agreed, due to its fragile nature, positioning within the trench and the time factor, that it would be safest to cut the boat into segments - a decision fully endorsed by Ted in the light of his experi-ences on the Humber foreshore.

Work on the boat continued for 13 hours each day and by Friday night all the recording had been completed ready for the lift on Saturday (pl.17.1). Working in conjunction with English Heritage conservators, the boat was cut into ten lettered sections using a diamond-tipped circular saw provided, complete with skilled operator, by the contractors, Norwest Holst. The lifting operation was difficult, with the time factor demanding some fairly desperate measures. Each cut section was freed from the sediment below by using trowels and water jets and then driving under horizontal wooden boards, keeping a thin layer of sediment between these and the ancient timber. Due to the presence of the enclosing cofferdam it was only possible to work from the east side. Once loose, each section was eased onto a pallet by up to nine people and then removed from the excavation using Dover Harbour Board's mobile crane. The timbers were taken by lorry to a water tank previously prepared nearby.

During the following week the contractors resumed work. It was clear that further portions of the vessel must lie to the north and south of the mid-section already lifted. Although these sections were beyond the limits of the contractor's excavations, fears increased regarding the effects on the surrounding water-table of the new water pumping station. There seemed no certainty that the remaining parts of the vessel would remain sufficiently waterlogged to allow long-term preservation. It was, therefore, decided to lift the other portions of the boat.

The close proximity of tall buildings immediately to the north precluded excavation here but a second cofferdam immediately to the south of the first was inserted and a further eight days allowed for the excavation of the southern section of the vessel. A further 3.5m of the craft was revealed including the remains of an original end.

The same general procedure was agreed for lifting and this was undertaken on the 19th October, with the benefit of previous experience and considerably easier access. By chance, the final day's work on the site (23rd October) corresponded precisely with the start date of the North Ferriby lifting programme in 1946! A total of 9.5m of the

Dover boat has been raised, which perhaps amounts to about one half to two-thirds of its full length.

Initial radiocarbon dates indicate that the boat is of the Middle Bronze Age, around 1350 BC. The construction details show that it was the product of a master boatbuilder working within a long established tradition. There seems little doubt that the craft was sea-going and it presumably made regular trips across the Dover Straits. It appears to have been old when abandoned in, or adjacent to, a freshwater channel eroded into peat. Sediments beneath the boat contain molluscs that show the presence of a stream with muddy banks covered with extensive vegeta-tion. Once abandoned, the boat infilled rapidly with tufa and was subsequently sealed by a thick layer of silt. Molluscs indicate this occurred within an environment dominated by damp open ground amongst small muddy pools or slowly moving streams. No definite evidence for brackish or saline water organisms has yet been found, despite the proximity to the present coast. In addition to a significant amount of lithic material, a rich assortment of palaeo-environmental data has been recovered from the boat and immediately adjacent contexts. Significant quan-tities of animal bone, largely from domestic cattle, were found.

Once conserved, it is hoped that the boat will be placed on permanent display at the new Dover Museum as from 1996.

## A significantly different sewn boat (VF)

The concentration of prehistoric sewn boats in the vicinity of the Humber Estuary and their absence from the British archaeological record elsewhere inevitably made it difficult to place the North Ferriby and Brigg boats in a context. For more than forty years they have stood alone in northern Europe, sole evidence, apart from Scandinavian

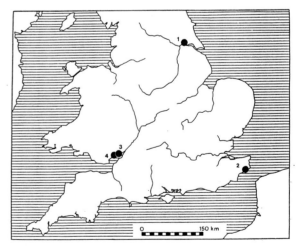

*Fig. 17.2 Distribution of sewn-plank boats in Britain; 1, North Ferriby; 2, Dover; 3, Caldicot; 4, Goldcliff*

rock-carvings (see paper 5), that vessels more elaborate than dugouts or skin boats were used for water transport in the Bronze Age. However, because they were found on the bank of a wide estuary it could not be determined if the

Ferriby boats had actually been seagoing, and sceptics confined their presumed role to that of local ferries.

Recent discoveries have constituted the long-awaited breakthrough in distribution and classification. The first was part of a Middle Bronze Age sewn-boat plank from Caldicot on the Severn Estuary (Parry & McGrail 1991) (see paper 16). This was followed by further finds of plank fragments at nearby Goldcliff in the summer of 1992 (Bell 1992) (see paper 2). Ted visited Caldicot and was naturally enthusiastic about the implications of the discovery, but this was nothing compared with his excitement in September 1992. He was then under doctor's orders to take things quietly and, as his driver for the day's visit to Dover, I planned to tend him carefully. This proved both impossible and unnecessary; his first sighting of the boat in the bottom of the first cofferdam galvanized him and he was down the ladder in a trice. No better tonic could have been devised and, after giving the team there the benefit of his long experience with the Ferriby boats, he talked about the find all the way home.

There certainly was much to talk about. The visible part of the boat posed many questions, the most immediate being the method used to keep the two parts of the bottom together (pl.17.1). There were no signs of any lashings or pegs, only mortises through which, apparently unwedged, transverse timbers passed. In addition to these there were pairs of large single cleats through which every fourth transverse timber also passed. Unlike Ferriby I the boat clearly had no keel-plank and each chine was formed by an ile-plank, L-shaped and carved out of an oak log.

Two cleats had been carved on the inside of the ile-planks. Since they did not relate to the bottom cleats and

had no attachments, we reasoned that they had perhaps been partnered by other cleats in a, now missing, upper strake. As at Ferriby the boat had been partly dismantled; cut lashings and a neat rabbet on the upper edge of each ile showed that there had been at least one additional strake each side. The withy stitches, apparently made from yew branches, were very familiar to Ted, but not the stopping material, beautifully preserved and visibly orange-brown, which plugged the stitch-holes (pl.17.2). Clearly the boat was much more lightly built than the Ferriby boats and originally very shapely.

The need to know what the ends of the boat were like was acute; thus Ted pronounced himself fit to drive as soon as there was a chance to see what had been revealed in the second cofferdam.

The construction was now much more clear (fig.17.3). Experience already gained had enabled excellent anticipatory measures to be taken, and within the very tight schedule the whole southern portion of the boat had been completely and neatly revealed. The most obvious feature was the continuance of the pattern of transverse timbers and what could now be recognised as long wedges. We were still no nearer to understanding how these had held the two halves of the hull together, and the 'secret' locking device was only revealed during lifting. On one of the pieces it was possible to glimpse the ridge left inside a mortise; this had deformed and tightly compressed a, presumably previously dried, wedge in place once it had taken up moisture and swelled (pl.17.3).

While excavating the second cofferdam we had all feared that the boat might be so long that it would extend beyond the far side, or worse still, be found to have been

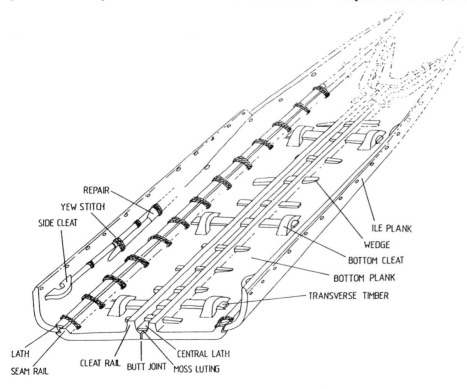

*Fig. 17.3 Diagram to show the components of the boat (Caroline Caldwell)*

destroyed by erosion just a short distance inside it. In the event the cofferdam fitted the boat beautifully and, as if by design, the pointed hood-ends of its iles terminated a convenient distance from the sheetpiling (pl.17.4). The rails, through which both wedges and transverse timbers passed, were seen to extend to the ends of the bottom-planks, but on a diverging course. Broad bevels formed the hood-ends of these bottom-planks and showed exactly where the missing end of the boat had once fitted. Large pads of moss luting and deliberately severed wedges proved that this part of the boat, too, had been dismantled in antiquity.

The find-spot of the boat, distant from a navigable river, implied that it was a truly seagoing vessel. It was certain to lend substance to models of cross-Channel trade based on discoveries of Continental artefacts, such as the tools and weapons from nearby Langdon Bay (Muckleroy 1980). Here was another quest, another boat to scrutinise, worry over, puzzle over and, above all, to cast new light on Ted's original discovery of a lifetime.

*Acknowledgements*. The raising of the Dover boat proved to be a splendid example of cooperation and assistance by many different companies, official bodies and individuals.

Substantial financial assistance was provided by English Heritage and the Department of Transport, whilst the engineers of Mott Macdonald and Norwest Holst gave invaluable practical help and encouragement on site. Dover Harbour Board played a vital part in the actual lifting and storage of the vessel, whilst Dover Museum and Dover District Council provided essential back-up to the excavators. The writers extend their sincere thanks to all concerned.

## References

Bell, M. 1992. Field Survey and excavation at Goldcliff 1992. *Severn Estuary Research Committee Annual report 1992*, 15-29.

Muckleroy, K. 1980. Two bronze age cargoes in British waters. *Antiquity* 54, 100-109.

Parry, S. and McGrail, S. 1991. A prehistoric boat fragment and a hard from Caldicot Castle Lake, Gwent, Wales. *Int. J. Naut. Archaeol.* 20, 321-324

**Plate 16.1-16.2**

*Pl. 16.1 Caldicot Castle Lake: site location in the Nedern Valley.*

*Pl. 16.2 Caldicot Castle Lake: middle Bronze Age boat strake.*

**Plate 16.3-16.4**

*Pl. 16.3  Caldicot Castle Lake: late Bronze Age pile alignment during excavation.*

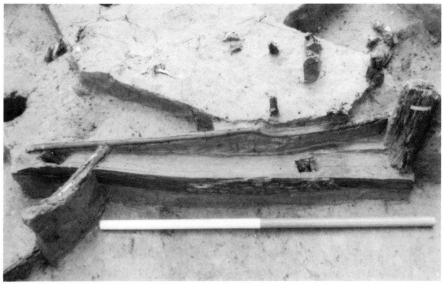

*Pl. 16.4  Caldicot Castle Lake: late Bronze Age radially split and double-mortised ash plank pegged into river-bed.*

**Plate 17.1-17.2**

*Pl. 17.1 The visitor's first sight of the Dover boat on 30th September 1992. Photo V. Fenwick.*

*Pl. 17.2 Details of a stitch and stopping. Photo A. Sargent.*

**Plate 17.3-17.4**

*Pl. 17.3 Piece of the boat after recovery. On the left, part of a wedge can be seen passing through a (broken) mortise. Photo A. Sargent.*

*P. 17.4 The remains of the boat in the second cofferdam. Note the truncated wedges which had secured the missing southern end and the beautiful tooling of the surfaces of the planks. Photo A. Sargent.*

**Plate 18.1-19.1**

*Pl. 18.1 Timber barn under construction. Note the 'pre-use' of roof timbers to support the main uprights.*

*Pl. 19.1 The ancient boat harbour of Suojoki in Keuruu seen from the south and from the mouth of the Suojoki River. The main excavation area of 1935 is c.15 metres to the north of the two men at the left. Photo S. Pälsi 1932.*

**Plate 19.2-19.3**

*Pl. 19.2 The excavations of 1935 in progress. Note the poles set crosswise on the stakes. Photo S. Pälsi 1935.*

*Pl. 19.3 Finds from Suojoki in Keuruu. From the left: an unidentified object, a piece of oar, two runners of toboggans (?) and a paddle. Photo S. Pälsi 1932.*

**Plate 20.1-20.2**

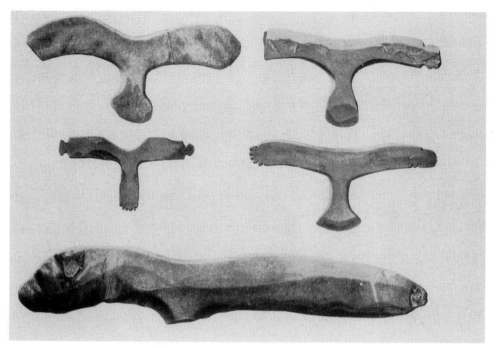

*Pl. 20.1 Types of T-formed implements (after Santesson 1941). Below is the* Tjärn *bear head.*

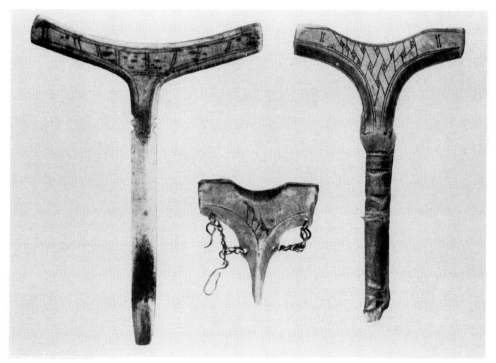

*Pl. 20.2 Saamish shaman* (noaidde) *drum hammer and pointer. The pointer shows the current figure painted on the drum skin after drumming. (After Santesson 1941).*

**Plate 20.3**

*Pl. 20.3 The boat-builder of a Saamish sewn boat in the village of Nuotjaur (Notozersk) on the Kola peninsula, Russia, in 1908 (after Hallström 1909). Note his T-formed implement, the wooden "hammer", Sam tjaukemvehtjer (tightening hammer) cr tjoarv-vehtjer (reindeer antler hammer), used to tighten the (pine) root fibre thread, while hammering in a treenail stopper. Photo Nordiska Museet Stockholm.*

# 18

# USE, RE-USE, OR PRE-USE?
## Aspects of the interpretation of ancient wood

### *Francis Pryor and Maisie Taylor*

This paper began life as a straightforward interim report on wood-working and toolmarks at Flag Fen, but while we were writing it, we started the construction of a timber barn, and this made us reconsider the way we were thinking about very much older timber. When we say 'we' we should add that the construction was actually carried out by two carpenters working for English Brothers Ltd., of Wisbech, one of the last British manufacturers of timber farm buildings.

Shortly after construction of the barn had started, we (and most other British wetland archaeologists) were kindly invited by the Canterbury Archaeological Trust to view the remains of the extraordinary Bronze Age boat that had recently been discovered at Dover. Of course Ted Wright was there, and of course we began to argue, to discuss and, best of all, to laugh a great deal. We were of the opinion that there was something rather odd - perhaps not altogether straightforward - about the depositional circumstances of the find, and Ted, doubtless quite rightly, thought some of our ideas were a bit odd. The resulting discussion was excellent value and ultimately led to this paper. We anticipate a rejoinder in the first mail following publication.

Consideration of the re-use (or pre-use) of timber led us to give much more thought to its actual *use*. Was the use of timber in prehistory always straightforwardly functional, and if not, what were the factors that might have influenced, or constrained, the way it was selected and employed within a particular structure? We will approach these general questions first; later we will examine a specific example of re- or pre-use at Flag Fen.

It is probably true to say that most trades and professions, even in the Britain of today, have quite an elaborate set of myths and taboos which often provide structure for on-the-spot decision making. For example, many farmers will not retain twin ewe lambs for future breeding purposes, sheep

tails are routinely docked and most ram lambs are castrated. All of these are practices which can be argued-against on what we have come to see as scientific, and indeed commercial or economic grounds. Yet they persist, almost universally. Perhaps the most myth-laden and dangerous of modern trades, is that of the maritime fisherman. One of us (FP) spent a month, some 30 years ago, working on a Grimsby trawler in disputed fishing-grounds off the north-east coast of Iceland. In addition to icebergs, storms and Icelandic gunboats, we had to contend with a web of traditional superstitions, beliefs and customs which were impossible for a callow youth to remember. Indeed, a trained ethnologist would have to have been on his or her mettle to have avoided causing offence to someone. The beliefs customs and taboos of the crew were usually to do with safety, the weather, the wife and family ashore, and catch-size or quality (the crew were paid a bonus which depended on the price the fish made on the quayside). In other words, these were the fishermen's principal concerns in life, and they found expression in many ways: some of the beliefs were associated with religion (it was considered very bad luck to set sail on Sunday) other were perhaps just superstitions. But all were treated, or so it seemed, as being equally important.

The sea has always been a dangerous place where elemental forces make mere humans feel insignificant; it was bad enough on a 250-foot diesel deep-sea trawler, but how much worse would it have been in a sewn boat - in a howling gale in the English Channel. It seems inconceivable that the life of a prehistoric mariner was not ruled by a most elaborate system of ideology, custom and practice. Yet this, cultural, aspect of the archaeology of boats is very rarely considered. The emphasis has always been upon boat-building technology and the craft's actual or theoretical handling capabilities. But what if the vessels had been built to be buried or beached? Did the Sutton Hoo vessel necessarily sail about in the North Sea? Did the vast

Hasholme logboat regularly ply the Humber? To answer these questions (which we will not attempt to do here) we must look beyond the boats and try to view them within their cultural contexts. They are boats, but they are also archaeological artefacts and boat, or maritime, archaeology is still a branch of general archaeology. Viewed thus, perhaps unexpected parallels for Hasholme may be found beneath the earthen barrows of Jutland, or indeed East Yorkshire (Mortimer 1905). Perhaps the *raison d' etre* for the Dover boat may not lie in its superb construction, but in the (deliberate?) removal of the transom board, the small, and perhaps temporary, stone 'landing stage', and the *bos* skull which presumably had been placed close by. There was other occupation debris nearby, but was it necessarily domestic? It is one thing to describe such material; it is quite another to explain its original deposition.

The objects found near the Dover boat could be straightforwardly explained as 'settlement debris', but that was also the explanation routinely given to the material found in the ditches of causewayed enclosures (eg Bamford 1985). At Etton we now believe that the rubbish in the pits and the 'debris' in the ditches were nothing of the sort; in both cases the material had been carefully placed in the ground, and often back-filled, during ritual ceremonies (Pryor, forthcoming). In that instance, it was the presence of the causewayed enclosure with its repeated associations with death, which led to the reinterpretation of the other, perhaps more mundane, data. This may also apply to boat finds. Everything depends upon one's initial point of view. If one considers that boats were treated as ordinary functional tools - as a means of getting from A to B whilst carrying a heavy load, C, then matters are archaeologically straightforward. If, on the other hand, one takes the view that a boat has always been treated as something out of the ordinary - a means of transport, yes, but also the vessel that carries souls across the Styx - then every new find should be treated with the utmost care; special efforts must then be made to understand how and why the vessel came to be deposited. We should not just assume that its loss was accidental. That must be proved. But as we have just noted, everything depends upon one's initial theoretical position.

The foregoing is a synopsis of our views which we discussed so stimulatingly with Ted at Dover. We were then writing the last chapters of the Etton report and were deeply within the grasp of Neolithic religion and ritual. Inevitably it coloured, perhaps unreasonably, everything we subsequently came to examine. To dig one large ritual site is unlucky, but to dig two is downright strange. At Flag Fen we first went for a straightforward domestic explanation (Pryor, French and Taylor 1986), but the discovery of over 300 deliberately broken bronzes and the realisation that the site was actively maintained for some 400 years, and was respected for another seven, or more, centuries, caused some major rethinking (Pryor 1992). The principal upshot of this reassessment was the recognition that Flag Fen was by no means straightforward; but whatever else

it might have been, domestic settlement it was not. Ritual again reared its head.

If maritime archaeology has been dominated by a rather specialised technological or naval architects' approach, then wetland archaeology has been carried out under the strong influences of wood technology and palaeoenvironmental research. Very often we have lost sight of the fact that water is not just the preferred medium of fish, or an obstacle to be traversed in order to get from A to B. Roads and tracks can link places together, but they can also form boundaries and allow people to pass between sometimes hostile territories on approved, safe, and even protected, routes. Perhaps offerings, such as the beautiful jadeite axe from the Sweet Track (Coles and Orme 1976) were placed in the ground at trackways to emphasise this boundary function. Perhaps, too, certain types of wood or timber were considered to be more appropriate for this purpose: the posts of the alignment at Flag Fen, which was most probably a major boundary, were largely in oak - always the strongest and most important British structural timber. But in the case of the Flag Fen post alignment, load-bearing strength was not needed; the rot-resistance of alder (which must have been in plentiful supply) would have made it more suited for the purpose, from a purely functional, cost-effective, point of view. These, one suspects, were not considerations that applied to the Bronze Age builders of Flag Fen.

There is a danger, however, in attempting to 'read' folkloric explanations into or from prehistoric wood. Unlike most of the structural materials that archaeologists are usually concerned with, wood was once alive and there are, and probably always were, rich traditions of folklore and legend associated with it (eg Baker 1980). So rich and diverse are these sources that it is perilous to attempt simplistic case-specific observations. It would perhaps be wiser to try and identify recurrent practices and to draw conclusions at a regional level. We will shortly discuss the somewhat extraordinary use of oak at Flag Fen, but striking examples, such as the use of purging buckthorn (*Rhamnus catharticus*) in a doorway to an Iron Age cattle stall at Assendelver Polders, Site Q, should also be noted (Therkorn *et al* 1984, 362). These are the perhaps obvious examples, but how many other times was wood selected for reasons other than its functional suitability? Perhaps the importance of culture in making such selections should be taken as read - or not, depending on one's theoretical position.

In many instances roads such as The Mall or the Appian Way can be major ceremonial monuments of themselves; in later prehistoric times, the great timber road at Corlea, also constructed of massive split oaks, was a signally unfunctional but very spectacular tribute to somebody's power and authority (Raftery 1990). One suspects that the Corlea chieftain's personal prestige slipped somewhat as the planks of his great road sank beneath the soft bog peats in their first Irish winter. Grand gestures, like major excavations, can go badly wrong. Like fire, water is also a potent symbol in its own right. Many of the sites found within it or around it must have been special. There is far more to the presence of corpses, swords, shields and spears within the bogs and fens of Bronze Age Europe than the dropping of coins into a fountain (Bradley 1990). Perhaps the placing of carefully-shaped, apparently 're-used' structural timbers within the make-up of the Flag Fen platform was more than just the casual re-use of wood as hard-core. Recent excavations have revealed four complete, unused or very lightly used quernstones in a small group lying directly beneath the lowest platform timbers. Surely this offering has no simple, functional, explanation? Similarly when we come to examine the bone data closely, and indeed the other metal and non-metal finds, we discover that their presence at Flag Fen must largely be attributed to non-domestic factors (Pryor and Chippindale 1992). Why should timber be any different? Like bronze it was a very valuable and useful commodity. Although rarely considered by prehistorians, it is possible that the control of timber resources was just as important as the control of ores, salt, amber or jet (Bradley 1984). There are, therefore, good reasons why timber should be involved in ritual activity.

We have seen that it was widely considered, by ourselves and others, from the very outset, that many of the Flag Fen timbers had been re-used (Pryor 1983). We will see shortly that this simple explanation does not accord with the complexity of the evidence, but first we should re-examine what we mean by the term re-use.

The idea of re-use has a firm grip in archaeology, perhaps as a result of the frequently observed practice on many excavations of robbing-out stone walls; the stone was then re- used in buildings somewhere else. Roman bricks may be found in Medieval churches; stone axes are often re-polished and Neolithic flint debitage lying on the surface was frequently re-worked in the Bronze Age (e.g. Mercer 1981); even Bronze Age metalwork can be ground-down and re-fashioned or, of course, simply melted and recast. By and large, however, metal or stone does not alter its workability when it is used. But wood does, and the process - seasoning - is irreversible.

Re-use does not have to involve modification of timber. Thus it is possible to remove a large oak beam from one building and use it in another. Provided the beam essentially rests on the top of a wall in one building, it may equally well perform the same task in another, without modification. If smaller structural timbers are involved, perhaps purlins or wall plates, then it may prove necessary to modify the timber prior to re-use. In the Bronze Age this would have to have involved the working of seasoned timber, probably oak, with bronze tools; experience at Flag Fen, using modern seasoned oak, suggests that this was almost impossible. Well-seasoned oak is so hard, and is so reluctant to split, that it is extremely difficult to re-work using bronze implements. Indeed, it is very difficult to achieve satisfactory results using a steel-edged tool! This led us to consider that in cases where timbers showed evidence for two episodes of working or use, the two episodes might have taken place within a relatively short span of time. If that were the case, both episodes of use might have involved green, readily workable, timber. This is where the new barn enters the story.

We were surprised when the timber for the barn was delivered by lorry on one day, and the two carpenters arrived in a small van on the next. There was no crane nor scaffolding. Holes were excavated for the twelve earthfast timbers which were placed upright, by hand, on two-foot-square concrete slabs to prevent them penetrating into the soft silts of the Fen. The post-holes were then backfilled without concrete. The upright, roof-support timbers were held in place by timbers that had yet to be incorporated into the structure. Purlins made the best temporary supports, as they had obliquely-cut scarf joints at one or both ends; these fitted snugly against the uprights (pl.18.1). The temporary supports were carried upon driven 2-inch square pegs at ground level. Numerous other timbers were used for temporary supports at various periods during the construction of the barn which did not require the use of any material that was not ultimately included in the final, completed, structure. Upon completion, the evidence that most of the barn roof timbers had been pre-used during the building's erection, consisted of a very few bent nails, and many nail-holes. In prehistoric times, in the absence of nails, the evidence for temporary pre-use might have consisted, for example, of a few (temporary) mortice-holes and the occasional piece of lashing twine.

The timbers at Flag Fen comprised a varied and inter-

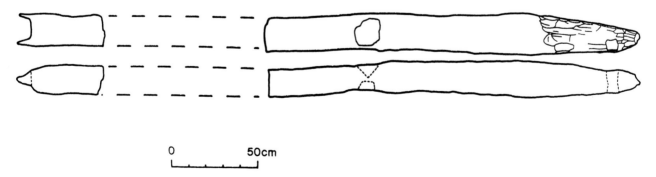

0                    50cm

*Fig.18.1  Outline drawing of a Bronze Age structural timber (B1421), in alder, from Flag Fen, showing at least two episodes of use. Note the mortice-like hole cut through the sharpened tip.*

esting assemblage and there is considerable evidence that certain pieces were used in more than one episode (Taylor 1992; Taylor and Pryor 1990). But there is much about the assemblage that is peculiar. Mortice holes may be unfinished and the apparently 're-used' timbers rarely show the signs of wear and tear that one might expect, had they been removed from derelict structures. One particular timber (fig.18.1) has a pencil-like sharpened tip and two 'ears' at its other end, which were probably intended to locate a roof rafter, or something similar (Taylor 1992, 483; see also Petrequin 1986, 71). The timber itself is alder (*Alnus glutinosa*), an unusual choice perhaps, and the tip shows no sign whatsoever of having been driven into the ground. Yet this apparently structural timber was clearly fashioned in at least two episodes; indeed, the second episode, which comprised two mortice-like holes half way along its length and one close to the tip, involved rather inferior craftsmanship and one of the mortice-holes had been left, incomplete. The hole at the tip makes no functional sense at all and other examples of this strange re-working have also been found at Flag Fen (e.g. Taylor 1992, fig. 7). One has to question whether this is indeed functional, or practical, re- or pre-use of timber.

At Etton, as at Flag Fen, there was overwhelming evidence, in the form of woodchips etc., for wood-working *in situ*. At that Neolithic site the debris indicated that small wood - coppice products and so forth - was being worked, but again, the archaeological remains were rather peculiar. There were very few finished products and it would appear that some of the 'debris' had in fact been selected or perhaps picked-over. There were also 'placed' deposits which had been left in the ground as offerings (Pryor, forthcoming). The Flag Fen evidence is different, in that far larger timber was involved, but it is hard to avoid the conclusion that, as at Etton, at least some of the *in situ* wood-working took place there *for its own sake*, and was not necessarily undertaken to make anything that would be of practical use elsewhere. Some of the structural timbers may have been removed from the houses of, for example, the recently deceased; but others clearly had a far more complex history to do, perhaps, with impermanent buildings erected on the platform for short-lived ritual purposes. Who knows, a few items may even have served a useful purpose!

Waterlogged wood has always been a difficult material to study, because, as Ted Wright has pointed out, the marks on its surface are so ephemeral and rarely survive conservation (Wright 1990). Given the extreme fragility of such data, we have tended, quite naturally, to concentrate our archaeological gaze on *minutiae*. Perhaps we should now lay aside our magnifying glasses and wonder not just how, but *why* prehistoric people worked wood with such enduring skill.

## References

Baker, M. 1980. *Discovering the folklore of plants*. Princes Risborough: Shire Books.

Bamford, H. 1985. *Briar Hill: Excavations 1974-1978*. Northampton: Development Corporation, Archaeological Monograph No. 3.

Bradley, R.J. 1984. *The social foundations of prehistoric Britain*. London: Longman.

Bradley, R.J. 1990. *The Passage of Arms*. Cambridge: University Press.

Coles, J.M. and Orme, B.J. 1976. The Sweet Track Railway Site. *Somerset Levels Papers* 2, 34-65.

Mercer, R.J. 1981. *Grimes Graves, Norfolk: Excavations 1971-72* 2 vols., Department of the Environment Archaeological Report No. 11. London: H.M.S.O.

Mortimer, J.R. 1905. *Forty Years' Researches in British and Saxon Burial Mounds of East Yorkshire*. London: Brown and Sons.

Petrequin, P. 1986. *Les sites littoreaux de Clairveax-les-Lacs (Jura)*. Paris: Editions de la Maison des Sciences de l'Homme.

Pryor, F.M.M. 1983. South-west Fen-edge survey, 1982/83: an interim report. *Northamptonshire Archaeology* 18, 165-9.

Pryor, F.M.M. 1991. *The English Heritage book of Flag Fen: prehistoric Fenland centre*. London: Batsford.

Pryor, F.M.M. 1992. Discussion: the Fengate/Northey landscape. *Antiquity* 66, 518-531.

Pryor, F.M.M. Forthcoming. *Excavations at Etton, near Maxey, Cambridgeshire, 1982-87*. English Heritage Archaeological Report. London.

Pryor, F.M.M. and Chippindale, C. (eds) 1992. Current Research at Flag Fen, Special Section. *Antiquity* 66, 439-57.

Pryor, F.M.M., French, C.A.I. and Taylor, M. 1985. An Interim Report on Excavations at Etton, Maxey, Cambridgeshire, 1982-1984. *Antiquaries Journal* 65, 275-311.

Pryor, F.M.M., French, C.A.I. and Taylor, M. 1986. Flag Fen, Fengate Peterborough I: Discovery, Reconnaissance and Initial Excavation (1982-85). *Proceedings of the Prehistoric Society* 52, 1-24.

Raftery, B. 1990. *Trackways through time*. Dublin: headline Publishing.

Taylor, M. 1992. Flag Fen: the wood. *Antiquity* 66, 476-98.

Taylor, M. and Pryor. F.M.M., 1990. Bronze Age building techniques at Flag Fen, Peterborough, England. *World Archaeology* 21, 425-434.

Therkorn, L.L., Brandt, R.W., Pals, J.P. and Taylor, M. 1984. An Early Iron Age farmstead: Site Q of the Assendelver Polders project. *Proceedings of the Prehistoric Society* 50, 351-73.

Wright, E.V. 1990. *The Ferriby Boats. Seacraft of the Bronze Age*. London: Routledge.

# 19

# SUOJOKI IN KEURUU
## An ancient boat harbour in Central Finland

*Janne Vilkuna, J.-P. Taavitsainen and Henry Forssell*

The number of lakes in Finland varies according to definition. The latest figure, presented in 1987, is 187 888, assuming a minimum area of 500 m² for bodies of water called lakes. At the same time, the number of rivers in Finland was also counted, with 647 as the total (Suomen Kuvalehti 24B/1987). In all, ten per cent of the area of Finland is covered by lakes. In view of this, Finland could be expected to provide a great deal of material on ancient watercraft. This is certainly true in theory, but boats have always been everyday objects, which may be why ancient watercraft and the collection of material have been somewhat neglected in research. There exist, however, finds that merit presentation and discussion. Presented in this connection is a project dealing with a site where mainly boats and related equipment have been found.

In the year 1930, while clearing peatland into field, the farmer Einari Uuttera found parts of an old boat at a depth of 70 cm near the shore of the Suojoki river discharging into a swampy bay at Suolahti in Keuruu, Central Finland (pl.19.1). The National Museum of Finland in Helsinki was informed of the find and the site was inspected by Dr Sakari Pälsi in 1932, in which connection a few other new finds were taken into safekeeping (pl.19.3). Newspaper and periodical clippings offer sensational information about the find, including estimates that the bog contained the remains of at least 50 boats and their equipment. The location, however, is an unlikely one for a find of this kind. The site is in a wilderness area in the parish of Keuruu, which is not one of the old central agricultural regions of Finland. Keuruu was not permanently settled until the end of the Middle Ages in the 16th century.

Three years later, in 1935, Pälsi and Auvo Hirsjärvi, also from the National Museum, conducted a small excavation at the site (pl.19.2). Field work was interrupted by war and lack of funds, but in 1952 Hirsjärvi and Esko Sarasmo from the Museum of Häme in Tampere continued work at the site with funding from a local historical society. The excavations lasted ten days, and an area of c.1000 m² was investigated (Hirsjärvi 1953; Jokipii 1959).

According to Hirsjärvi (1952) the excavations showed that the area containing finds was very large, consisting of three smaller areas along the riverside with a distance of 170 metres between the outermost parts (fig. 19.1). The original finds were from the middle area, 44 metres from the river. Because this part was under cultivation in 1952, only one end of a field strip could be opened. In addition, the sides of ditches were examined, and random checks were made. The middle area proved to be the richest part. The south area was on the boundary of the property near the mouth of the river and only three metres from its bank. Pälsi and Hirsjärvi had excavated there in 1935, and it was completely opened in 1952. The north area was c. 34 metres from the river and some 54 metres from the middle area. Stray finds were recovered at various intervals between the three areas.

The finds were mostly parts of boats: keel timbers, fores, staves, strakes, oars, paddles, oarlocks, poles, etc. Also found were winter transport equipment: skis and parts of sledges or toboggans of the *ahkio*-type. In addition, a decorated birch-bark vessel (Pälsi 1934) and pieces of unidentified objects were found.

As there are no excavation reports, it has been difficult to critically evaluate the information usually presented of the site. The data are gleaned from newspaper and periodical clippings, a brief note on the 1952 excavations (Hirsjärvi 1953), photographs, and a number of articles where some of the finds are discussed (see e.g. Itkonen 1937, 72-73). Sources previously believed missing have now come to light. At the end of 1992 a museum find was made: the plan

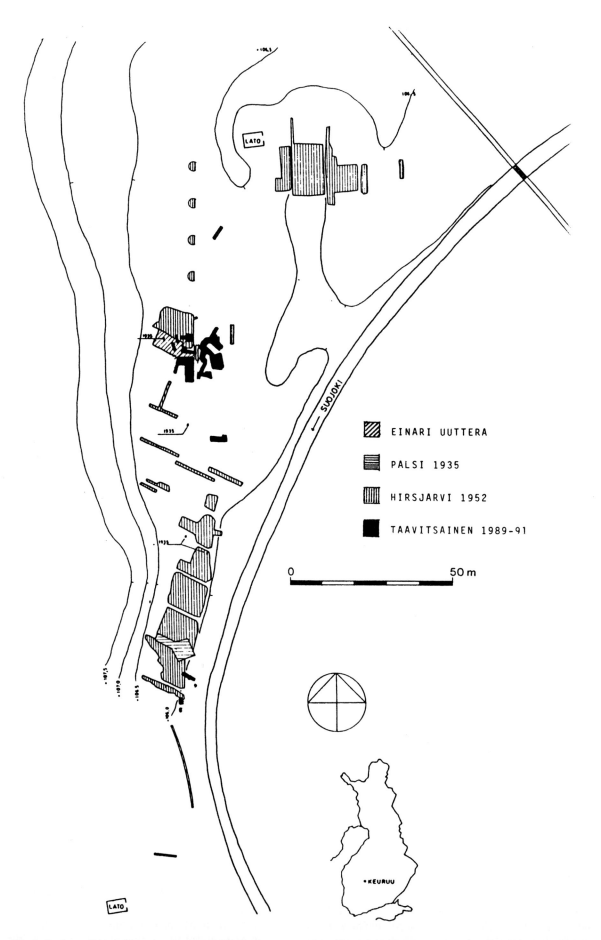

*Fig. 19. 1 A plan of the excavation areas of different years in Suojoki in Keuruu, Central Finland. Drawing S. Rintala.*

and maps of the excavation areas, many detail drawings of finds and photo negatives, but no reports of the excavations of 1935 and 1952. In spite of their scanty nature, these documents will, however, help to check some of the information, e.g. the possibly overestimated number of boats cited above.

The Suojoki finds from the 1930s and '50s are in the collections of the National Museum of Finland (Helsinki), the Museum of Häme (Tampere), the Museum of Central Finland (Jyväskylä) and in the gate building of the Keuruu churchyard wall.

Of these finds, the boats have been the subject of most attention (Forssell 1986). Their construction technique was quite unknown to Finnish scholars of the period. A distinctive feature of these boats is the lack of iron nails; roots were used to bind the strakes and other parts of the boat. This is called the sewing or binding technique. The boat consists of five parts: a hollowed-out keel timber that has been spread out, hollowed-out fore and aft staves, and two side strakes. In Scandinavian ethnology, the construction has given rise to the term "five-part" boat (Sw. *femdelsbåt*). This type is regarded as an intermediary stage in the development of the clinker-built boat from the dug-out to the stave-constructed type with several clinker-built strakes.

Archaeological finds of organic materials are rare in Finland, which is somewhat astonishing in a country where a third of the land area is covered with peat. Consequently, the dating of the Suojoki find posed a number of problems. The finds, and especially the decorated birch-bark vessel, suggest a dating to the period of transition from the Iron Age and to the Middle Ages (according to the Finnish chronology), however no later than the 13th century. Later, two radiocarbon ages have been obtained for one of the boats (NM 7791:1). When calibrated, they place it most probably at the end of the 13th century (Hel-36 BP 730±130, one sigma cal AD 1180 (1272) 1389 and Hel-37 BP 670±120, one sigma cal AD 1250 (1285) 1400; calibration according to Stuiver and Pearson 1986).

The Suojoki site has been called an ancient boat harbour and linked with the *pirkkalaiset*, medieval peasants and farmers of the settled areas who traded with the Lapps and exacted tribute from them (e.g. Hirsjärvi, 1950 53).

In his research in the 1980s on sewn boats, Henry Forssell examined all the Suojoki finds in museum collections, and became interested in the site. It was obvious that there was more material in the bog. He contacted the Museum of Central Finland in Jyväskylä, and in the spring of 1988 Forssell and Janne Vilkuna of the Museum visited the site, which was no longer under cultivation and was completely inundated by the spring flood. A local, who had participated in the 1952 excavations acted as guide. He told the researchers that when ditches were dug a few years earlier, boards had risen from the bog.

In August 1989, a one-week trial excavation was carried out under the direction of J.-P. Taavitsainen of the National Board of Antiquities and Janne Vilkuna of the Museum of Central Finland. The preliminary goal was to locate the previously excavated areas in the swampy bay, which was now becoming overgrown with grass and willows. The locals who had participated in the excavations of the 1930s and '50s helped, but test pits in places indicated by them did not reveal any finds. Comparatively recent ditches proved to be better locations. A piece of *ahkio* keel was found at the edge of a ditch and probes revealed hard wood in many places. These observations pinpointed the location of the middle area. The lack of excavation reports and plans posed a great deal of difficulties for the excavation team. There was a risk that previously excavated areas would be re-excavated, as it was unknown whether all the finds were taken to museum collections or not.

The Museum of Central Finland and the National Board of Antiquities have collaborated in a number of minor projects concerning the Iron Age settlement history of Central Finland (see Vilkuna 1982; Taavitsainen 1990). As the Early Medieval Suojoki site added to the results of previous work, a project was organized for studying the site.

As both the National Board of Antiquities and the Museum of Central Finland lack funds for specific problem-oriented excavations, such ventures have to be improvised. Like the field work in the earlier projects, the present one also relies on volunteers, including Soviet archaeologists (1991). The local historical society has provided indispensable help for the Suojoki project as well as the grants from the Fund for Central Finland of the Finnish Cultural Foundation and the Centenary Fund of the *Helsingin Sanomat Daily*. Because of limited resources, the field seasons have been very short: one week in 1990, and two weeks in 1991. In 1992 measurements for mapping the plan were made. Compared with the earlier excavations, excavated areas have been very modest.

The main objective has been to define the nature of the find site. The finds were of the same character as previously (fig. 19.2). During the excavations the overall extent of the site was discovered to be the same as previously reported except that no finds were made in the northern area. This was, however, the most difficult area to localize without maps in an environment without any fixed points. Samples for radiocarbon dating were collected from three areas (southern, middle, and an area between the middle and northern ones) to check for possible contemporaneity or chronological succession. There would also be opportunities for dendrochronological dating, but the lack of funds prevent using this dating method extensively.

After being photographed and documented, the finds were left in the bog, except for a few artefacts taken to the Museum of Central Finland for exhibition purposes. This can, of course, be criticized, but the reason for it is very simple - the lack of adequate conservation facilities.

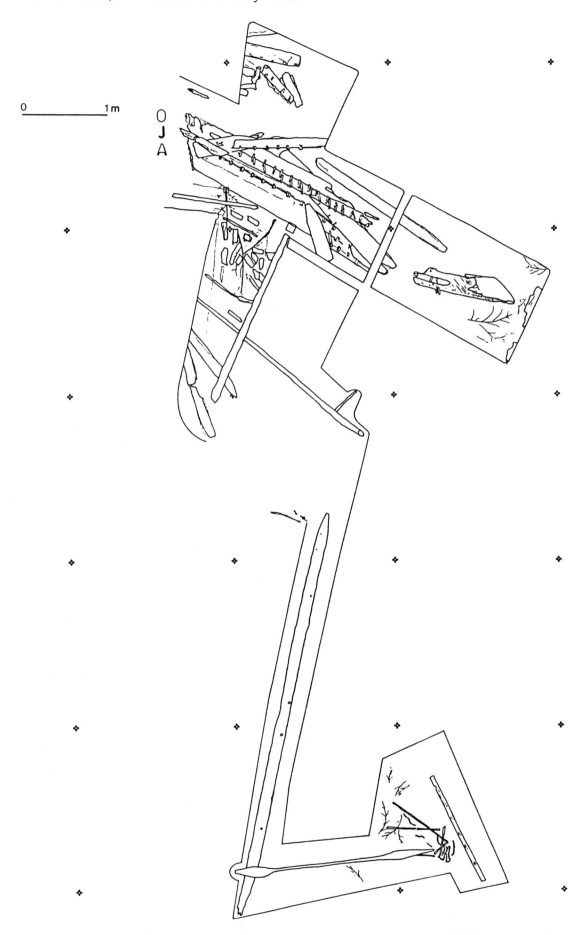

*Fig. 19.2  A detail plan of parts of the central area. Drawing V. A. Nasarenko 1991.*

The Suojoki project deals with the following problems:

1) The reconstruction of the site's lacustrine environment and its flora at the time of use.

2) Additional information on the material culture of a period which is poorly known archaeologically. These rare finds of organic materials will provide an exceptional perspective on the material culture of the period, and especially the development of the "five-part" boat.

3) A detailed discussion of the archaeological formation processes operating in the context. In other words, how and why did the finds get into the shore bog and become preserved? Was this due to religious or purely utilitarian practices? Our working hypothesis is that the material was timber stored for re-use by a foraging population (see pl.19.2).

4) The connections of the site with local settlement and its role in the settlement processes of the wilderness area.

The last problem requires more presentation. One of the major questions is where were settlements located. So far, no dwelling sites have been discovered in the vicinity, which makes the project to some extent incomplete. Was Suojoki possibly a terminus or an intermediate point on a wilderness route? These are difficult subjects, as there are few Iron Age finds from Keuruu, and the earliest historical sources are from the beginning of the 16th century. Only three oval striking stones of the Early and Middle Iron Age and one Late Iron Age find, consisting of a fire steel, an oval tortoise brooch of Savo-Karelian type and a long iron artefact, are known in Keuruu. The last-mentioned find was made in 1875 in the village of Lihjamo *c*.4,3 kilometres northeast of Suojoki. It may have connections with the Suojoki site.

One of the special problems of settlement history is posed by the economic structures of the Iron Age, in other words the relationship between the trader peasants of the settled areas of Häme and the representatives of the foraging culture of the interior, the Lapps (see e.g. Taavitsainen 1988).

Here, a phenomenon called *eränkäynti*, the Finnish practice of wilderness hunting and resource utilization, as described in written sources from medieval and modern times, is used as a loose model. It is briefly described by the historian Armas Luukko (1959 40; on *eränkäynti* see also e.g. Jokipii 1966) as follows:

> " Wilderness resources were of major importance for the medieval economy of Finland. Even in the old localities of settlement the farmers did not limit their activities to cultivation and animal husbandry, but strove towards an effective use of the opportunities for hunting and fishing provided by the land. Because of Finland's numerous lakes and the long water routes, wilderness areas could be taken into use which were even as far as 250-300 kilometres

from the home regions. The wilderness tracts were often private property and could be inherited, sold, exchanged or forwarded in other ways. The separation of such an area with its fishing waters from an original holding is mentioned in a document from 1390, referring to a donation by Magnus Kase, bailiff of the Castle of Häme, to the Cathedral of Turku. The bailiff donated to the cathedral the Kantala holding in the parish of Saarioinen (Häme) with the explicit exception of the "squirrel forests", fishing waters and the Lapps to the north in Bothnia, which belonged to the holding. "

Suojoki must have been, in one way or another, a meeting place of the farmers and the Lapps, these two economically different cultures mentioned in historical sources concerning the *eränkäynti* phenomenon.

Both winter and summer vehicles are represented in the find material, and it is probable that the place is a "home port". The boats were naturally serviced at the home harbour. A boat in bad condition was not used to carry precious loads, but it could be used for a long time on the home lake as a fishing boat. This supports the Lapp nature of the site. It is perhaps worth mentioning that one of the products which the Lapps of the later days in Lapland transported to the settled areas were parts of boats (Itkonen 1948, 219; see also Westerdahl 1987, 82).

Finally, an analysis of place-names as well as pollen analyses of bogs or small lake sediments will be needed to shed more light on settlement history and land use in the Keuruu area. The collaboration of a toponymist and palynologists is desirable.

Pollen analyses from Keuruu and, for comparison, also from other places in Central Finland are now in progress, and most of the radiocarbon datings have been completed. They point to the same direction as the earlier ones. The exception is the southern area uncovered in 1991 which obviously belongs to the 15th and 16th centuries, a period when Keuruu according to historical sources received its permanent farming population. The analysis of the newly found maps has also begun. A disturbing observation was made on the basis of the plan: it seems as if some of our excavation areas in the middle area had already been excavated in 1952. There were, however, no signs of disturbance in the peat sediments overlaying the finds excavated in 1989-91. Due to the lack of written comments on the maps we do not know whether all the excavation areas were totally excavated or not. The analysis of detail on the plans will help solve this problem. Much work is, however, still needed for final results to emerge. After a few years we hope to tell more about the history of watercraft in the northern coniferous zone of Eurasia and its role in the settlement historical processes of this area.

*Janne Vilkuna, J.-P. Taavitsainen & Henry Forssell*

## References

Forssell, Henry 1986. Keuruun venelöydöt. *Keski-Suomi* 18, 18-28.

Hirsjärvi, Auvo 1953. Muinaisten erämiesten jäämistöä Keuruulta. *Kotiseutu* 1/1953, 47-50.

Itkonen, T. I. 1937. Muinaissuksia ja -jalaksia IV. *Suomen Museo* 1936, 66-83.

Itkonen, T. I. 1948. *Suomen lappalaiset vuoteen 1945* II. Helsinki.

Jokipii, Mauno 1959. Vanhan Ruoveden pitäjän historia eräkaudesta isoonvihaan. *Vanhan Ruoveden historia* I, 133-138.

Jokipii, Mauno 1966. Die mittelalterliche finnische Erä-Kultur. *Wissenschaftliche Zeitschrift der Ernst-Moritz-Arndt-Universität Greifswald*. Jahrgang XV. *Gesellschafts- und sprachwissen- schaftliche Reihe* Nr 1, 53-64.

Luukko, Armas 1959. Erämark. *Kulturhistoriskt lexikon för nordisk medeltid* IV, 39-45.

Pälsi, Sakari 1934. Keuruun suolöydön koristetut tuohet. Excavationes et studia. Opuscula in honorem Alfred Hackman 14.10.1934. *Suomen Muinaismuistoyhdistyksen Aikakauskirja* XL, 215-222.

Stuiver, Minze & Pearson, Gordon W. 1986. High-precision Calibration of the Radiocarbon Time Scale AD 1950 - 500 BC. *Radiocarbon* 28, No. 2B, 805-838.

Taavitsainen, J.-P. 1988. Wide-Range Hunting and Swidden Cultivation as Prerequisites of Iron Age Colonization of Finland. *Suomen antropologi* 4/1987, 213-233.

Taavitsainen, J.-P. 1990. Ancient Hillforts of Finland. Problems of Analysis, Chronology and Interpretation with Special Reference to the Hillfort of Kuhmoinen. *Suomen Muinaismuistoyhdis- tyksen Aikakauskirja* 94.

Vilkuna, Janne 1982. Konginkankaan Pyhäsalon varhaismetallikautinen hautaröykkiö. *Keski-Suomi* 17, 229-234.

Westerdahl, Christer 1987. "Et sätt som liknar them uti theras öfriga lefnadsart". Om äldre samiskt båtbygge och samisk båthantering. *Skrifter utgivna av Johan Nordlander-sällskapet* 11.

# 20

# LINKS BETWEEN SEA AND LAND

## *Christer Westerdahl*

The scientific works associated with Ted Wright illustrate his tireless quest for new and stout knowledge in our special field of early boats. In 1984 he published some experiments in boat stitching on the evidence of an implement possibly directly connected with the building of the Ferriby Boats (fig. 20.1) My principal area for investigation was at that time northern Scandinavia, where a tradition of sewn boats, especially among the Saami, is a fairly well-known cultural trait. One of the great advantages with this area is that many such traits have been in existence in comparatively late times, whereas they have disappeared elsewhere. The common designation for such traits is of course survivals, but I would like to point out that I do not share the likewise common view that such survivals would mainly represent the general backwardness of the region. Instead I would rather try to emphasize the functional and traditional character of these survivals. They are the products of adaptation and also carry a cultural connotation which may even be related to processes of (mostly ethnic) identity. Still, the same feeling pervaded me as a southerner once in 1969 as Olaus Magnus in the beginnings of the 16th century: "His great experience was to find that the farther he travelled northward in space, the farther he travelled backward in time" (Granlund 1972:9).

The deliberations carried out by Ted Wright in the beginning of the 1980s gave me new impetus for reconsidering old material. The outcome of this discussion is not to present an obvious case but to pin-point certain aspects of a rather unaccounted-for problem.

## The status of boat-builders

One of the questions posed here concerns the comparatively high status of the boatbuilder in ancient societies. We must, however, not imagine them as specialized arti-

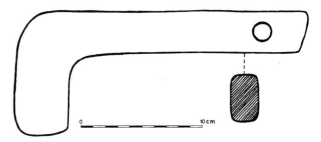

*Fig. 20.1 Sketch of an artifact found near Ferriby boat n° 2 (after Wright 1984)*

sans of the kind firstly formally indicated by the medieval guilds. Rather it appears that the boatbuilders exerted their prestige in combination with other handicrafts and other social activities, e.g. contemporary forms of trading. The sources mainly concern Europe in the Early Middle Ages. Ethnographical parallels have not been explicitly invoked but they would certainly confirm a similar, but not necessarily individualized, status role (note 1).

## Implements of T-form

This discussion concerns a very distant past, as compared to the sources, to which have been referred above.

The T-formed implements of reddish brown slate have long been a mystery to northern archaeologists, without conclusive evidence as to their function. However, as their distribution shows, they remain rather a regional phenomenon, encompassing only a section of the Bothnian area of Sweden and Finland (fig. 20.2). On the present Swedish side they have been found in an area, roughly the coastal and northern part of the province of Ångermanland, where northern/eastern and southern/western cultural elements overlap, from Neolithic times up to historical times, in what was a cultural border zone (e.g. Westerdahl 1989). In

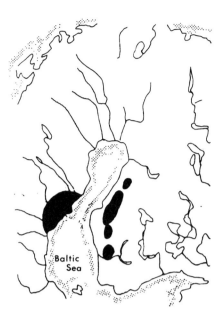

*Fig. 20.2 The distribution of T-formed implements (after Westerdahl 1985).*

this light they seem to constitute one of the very few material signs of provincial autonomy. However the "slate culture" that they represent is spread over a much large area of Fennoscandia than the Bothnian Gulf proper. It also appears that the pictorial or formal elements inherent in their character covers an extensive field in space as well as in time.

Around 60% (more than 30) of all T-formed implements have been found in one single settlement site, *Överveda* in the parish of Nordingrå, Ångermanland. It seems that the kind of rock used has a local origin, the mountain of *Ringkalleberg* in the same parish. It is often called slate, but in reality it might as well be described as a fine-grained sandstone (*cf* Karman 1989). In the same province have been found another dozen, of approximately the same material, and probably mostly at settlements at the same level, *c* .70 m above sea level and a little more, corresponding to a shore-line of 3000-3500 B.C. Perhaps half a dozen finds originate on the other side of the Bothnian Gulf, where the effects of the land rise in this shallow plain represent far greater changes in land contours than in the mountainous and steep west. Thus, these settlements now lie far inland. A few other loose find sites spread out towards the mountain chain further west and along the Norrland coast. Accordingly, the general milieu of the T-formed implements seem to be maritime, a fact that has curiously enough not been taken into account by most scholars dealing with this subject.

The general form and size of the T-formed elements is one clearly adapted to the human hand, 10-15 cm x 5-7 cm (pl.20.1). But it was to some extent an irregular find of T-formed implement, the bearhead sculpture of *Tjärn*, parish of Arnäs, Ångermanland (pl.20.1, below), which started the discussion on their function. This sculpture is larger and more three-dimensional in shape than the others, but it has a protruding base, although broken off

(maybe in the process of manufacture, since the sculpture seems not to have been polished, in contrast to other implements or related slate objects) betraying a close relationship to the T-formed elements. The Tjärn head is certainly an amalgamation of two classes of artifacts. The other close relationship is that to elk- and bear-headed axes of mainly eastern emphasis, Carelia, Finland but also Russia. Only a very few represent bears like the Tjärn case. There are several other finds of animal-head axes on the eastern seaboard of Sweden, including the beautiful elk head from *Alunda*, Uppland. Most are ceremonial or status axes of no practical value, provided with shaft holes where the bear head of Tjärn has its (intended) downward projection. The implications of the above-mentioned cultural connections in this huge area have not been fully understood. It may very well be that a world of ecological and cultural similarity is reflected in the religious character of the objects.

The northern Swedish field archeologist O B Santesson compared the T-formed implements with Saamish shaman drum "hammers" (here pl.20.2; Santesson 1941). His explanation of their form was that they were both magical objects. Several other authors have since dealt with the subject (note 2).

However, as a summary of their talented efforts, the different arguments put forward to discern one single function overlook the fact that the singular traits of the T-formed implements do not encourage the notion of a homogenous group destined for one purpose only. There are objects with clear-cut indentations, but only a very few. There are some with scraper heads, but by no means all contain such traits. The only constant and recurring feature is in fact their form, well pointed out in the neutral group name *T-formed implements*. It seems therefore, in my opinion, more rewarding to look for combined purposes, where the form may reveal a possible original feature, maybe in another material which in this case certainly brings us closest to the cross-formed features of antler. Furthermore, the context of the excavated settlement finds at Överveda also reveals that the more or less every-day function of the implements (and possibly their prototypes in another material) cannot exclusively belong to the magical sphere.

*Seal-hunting culture*

The question posed by Almgren on the most important prey animals of the hunter-gatherer culture with the T-formed implements was an important step forward, but not in the sense of the author's own argument. Almgren proposes elk and reindeer. Reindeer was, by the way, very sparse in Norrland at this time, most probably even non-existent in this area. Elk is certainly the most important prey inland. Recovered osteological material (burnt bones) from the coastal settlement at Överveda clearly shows that the animal hunted was the ringed seal *Pusa hispida*. This must reasonably mean that the sealing economy of the coastal area explains the distribution of the T-formed implements. It may be that the inland occurrences of these objects indicate a seasonal character of the sealing activities, also apparent in other archeological features inland, referring to particular seasons of the year for different activities. The general explanation offered by Baudou (1992, 79f) for the Överveda settlement is that of autumn net hunting, since a small number of stones, interpreted as net sinkers of appropriate sizes, have been found at the site. But the exclusive occurrence of ringed seal bones at Överveda may not mean that other species of seals were uninteresting. It only indicates that the ringed seal went to the settlement in larger chunks than others, and presumably for at least some food.

The ringed seal is relatively small, rather shy, and appears mostly in small family groups. When feeding near land, together with its cubs born on the ice in the early spring, it can often swim up outlets of rivers or bays into the interior. In such narrow waters it can either be caught in stationary nets or closed in by such traps rapidly put out by wary hunters. Recent experiences appear to indicate autumn as a suitable time for such hunting practices. At the same time of the year, according to recent tradition, the grey seals could be hunted in the night at customary resting places, seal boulders, with long harpoons in boats from the seaside. All animals are at their fattest in the autumn, preparing for the lean months of winter. But genuine blubber consumption, of which there is little evidence, would probably have focused interest on other seal species than the ringed seal.

However, prehistoric finds from the Bothnian indicate that the ringed seal also has been hunted with harpoons (Oulojoki, Finland). Several finds show clearly that the Greenland seal, *Phoca groenlandica*, with the most beautiful skin of all the known seal species, but now extinct in the Baltic, was hunted in this way. Several skeletons with harpoons have been found. Dating is difficult or non-existent, but would at least mean the Stone Age. Ringed seals and Greenland seals presumably were taken for their skins. To get winter clothes the ringed seal seems to provide the most pliable and workable skins of all available animals.

Part of the background of hunting at Överveda may be this ecological pattern. However, the efficient use of these resources may mean that other times of the year were as active as autumn, particularly the early spring. In this world it seems obvious that boats have been used. The distribution of the T-formed implements on the other side of the Baltic gives another indication of sea-borne communications. The fairly warm climate of the period may also have made it difficult to find unbroken ice for sea-crossings (note 3).

Besides, the extensive transports in the area to and from the common riverine settlements inland to the coast in an established seasonal pattern seem strongly to encourage the view that boats were an essential element in the economy. This also means that the social role of the Boat ought to have been emphasized in the world of belief, ritual and symbolism.

The immediate impression of the form of the T-formed implements is that of a device for tightening some thread-like material. By applying the human hand to the levers of the implement and efficiently stopping the material from slipping off the three protruding wings it would be possible to stabilize the thread in a tightening position for a certain purpose. The purpose could have been the application of a stopper in a seam. In my proposed version, which refers to another type of stitch than in the Ferriby boats, that of running stitches, this is done on a log boat, where a small treenail stopper is driven in at the seam hole. The current comparison is made with a Saamish boat builder on the Kola peninsula as illustrated by Gustaf Hallström in 1908 (pl.20.3). The current implement cannot reasonably, as far as I know, be combined with sewing in textile or skin material, even if the closest and very tempting alternative to a log boat would be a seal skin canoe (note 4).

## The social and symbolic picture

Variations of traits of the T-formed implements imply that the hunter-gatherer culture allowed the personal imprint on this object. The boat-builder emphasized either the scraper, like the late Inuit *ulo* knife (fig. 20.3) or the indented stamps (Almgren proposal) or some other feature. The prestige of the boat-builder, i.e. the head of

*Fig. 20.3 Sketch of the use of an Inuit* ulo *scraper knife.*

a family group, is inherent in the conclusion that the implement originally was made in another material and that a translation may have been made in another material, possibly considered more durable. It cannot, however, be denied that bird-oriented associations of the shamanistic traditions may have influenced the proportions of the devices. We have become more aware of such timeless archetypes in later years. Thus, it may be that Hallström too harshly condemned the huge time perspectives of Santesson (note 5).

I am inclined to propose that the Överveda groups were

headed by men enhancing their prestige in a profoundly fragmented social system by signs combined in the implements of the T-formed type. Trying to imagine their other properties I would see these men as the ritual leaders. The Saami shaman, *noaidde (nåjd)*, of later times functioned in fragmented groups of a similar character, although distant in time. They were not in any sense specialized priests, they were simply, but not simplistically, heads of the *sidda (sita)*, extended family groups with retainers or related small combined communities. I suggest that this was also the case in Neolithic times, when Norrland shows signs of an culturally *autonomous* development, in contrast to other periods, according to Baudou (1992).

The impressive contemporary rock carvings of the Nämforsen rapids in the same province, the most extensive in northern Sweden, display a number of symbols of a related kind to the bird forms of the T-formed implements, notably elks and boats, in some isolated case a salmon. The people of the Överveda and other coastal sites (*c*. 10 approximately contemporary ones are known along this coast) may have met other inland culture groups at the large summer settlement of Nämforsen, a central place for collective ritual embodied in the rock carvings. A pattern of such meeting places with rock carvings, at mighty rapids close to the outlets of the major river systems, may have been established after the Nämforsen prototype in Upper Norrland.

It is obvious that the pictorial repertory of Nämforsen and possibly the environment of the T-formed implements consciously avoid the current prey animals. The salmon was the likely prey in spring and summer time at Nämforsen whereas the seals were the dominant objective of the autumn or late winter Överveda settlement.

This makes for structural considerations. In a system of oppositions these symbols may have worked as repositories of meaning, transcending the immediate reality. These oppositions include the following basic "elements":

air
water
earth
sky

I suggest that the shamans were considered the human links between such fields of action or elements. But also the animal (e.g. the seal) or a plant (e.g. the rowan) could be links in a structured popular belief (note 6).

The foremost animal link between air and earth, sky and land, is the bird. This is undoubtedly an archetype. The air and the sky may have been represented by the elk. There are several Siberian/ Eastern mythologies where Cosmos is built on a huge elk (Taavitsainen 1978; Tilley 1991, 126f).

On the other hand the boat existed and was used between land and sea -thus a slight departure from the dichotomy of earth and water. It was a creation of culture (Man and Cosmos), with the purpose of conquering Nature (ie the

unstructured Chaos). Like the other links it had properties derived from both worlds, both culture and nature. It was made in land but tossed about amongst the waves. The boat and its contents is always at the grace of the elements (Kobylinski 1988; Carpenter 1991). It is to sea and land what a bird represents to air and earth.

So I believe that the tightening device and combined implement in bird form may ultimately have indicated both the shaman/boatbuilders métier and his *faber pontifex/ navifex* status, creating bridges spanning the elements and dichotomies of the known world. And the closest animal companion of the boat not only in its status as a link between sea and land, but also in a more practical sense, is in fact the seal, the principal prey of the wielders of T-formed implements.

## Notes

1. In Norse literary material (*c*.1200 AD) the concept and title "stemsmith" (*stafnasmidr*) is emphasized, suggesting that the other elements of construction were left to what was considered (at least in posterity) to be inferior and anonymous people. The famous passage in the Saga of the Norwegian king Olaf Tryggvason (88; Snorri Sturlason; Hødnebø/Magerøy 1979: 186f, Adalbjarnarsson (ed) 1979: 335f) mentions the name of an individualized *stafnasmidr*, Torberg Skavhögg, leading the work on the huge "Orm inn langi" (The Long Serpent).

   In archaeological material the context of some grave finds may mean additional arguments to consider a particular status among boatbuilders in their local group. (*Hérouvillete*, Calvados/ Normandie, France, grave no. 10, 500-550 AD, Decaens 1971: 83ff; the (osteologically) Saamish boat-grave of Scandinavian tradition at *Lekanger*, Gildeskål, Salten, Norway, 10th century AD; Stenvik 1980, Westerdahl 1987: 31). Besides, implement finds of the *Mästerby* kind (Gotland; *c*.1000 AD, Arwidsson/Berg 1983) and others, although less complete (the *Staraja Ladoga* find of Russia, middle of the 8th century AD, is rather inconclusive as to its connections with boatbuilding) gives a good picture of the many-sided activities of the smith.

2. Åke Ohlmarks somewhat later went along the same route and pointed out their bird form, connecting them with the shamanist belief of the soul of the magician travelling in this form to other worlds (Ohlmarks 1947). Gustaf Hallström criticized Santesson's view by emphasizing the enormous time span between T-formed implements and the known Saamish shaman drums (Hallström 1941). He would rather think of knife-scrapers for hides. But the comparisons used were still extended in time and space, and fairly little put in relation to ecology and culture. Another valuable development of this function was presented by Bertil Almgren (Almgren 1957), who in particular had observed the indentations on several (though not all) implements and interpreted them, on the evidence of recent ethnographical parallells (Inuit), as stamps for ornaments in skin. It may appear remarkable that such a material as slate stone was used considering the fact that antler, horn or bone would be abundantly available in hunter-gatherer cultures. But slate/sandstone of the T-formed variety is unusually easy to work, even to some extent easier than e.g. antler.

3. Consequently, clubbing on the ice of grey seal and Greenland cubs may not have been of current interest, except now and then in late winter.

4. A curious parallel to precisely shaman drum hammers is indicated by the Saamish word for this hammer, which is not a hammer at all *vehtjer* or *tjaukemvjetjer*, i.e. hammer, tightening hammer. In spite of its being made of wood it is also called *tjoarv-vehtjer*, i.e. reindeer antler hammer (Westerdahl 1987: 14).

5. The time span has anyway been reduced by the fact that the first reindeer antler T-formed implements (pointed out already by Santesson 1941) from Kjelmøy, Varanger, N Norway have now been dated as early as *c*. 800-500 BC, i.e. partly Late Bronze Age; *cf* Solberg 1910.

6. Rowena Farre has an excellent description of later time Celtic folk belief in Scotland on such links in her fascinating book dedicated to a young harbour seal (Farre 1954). There seem to be common elements with rural Scandinavia, although parallells may be hard to establish, owing to sparse material on a system in the north. But the same animals and plants figure in the north as in Scotland, sometimes allegedly for different reasons.

# References

Adalbjarnarson, B. (ed) 1979. Snorri Sturluson Heimskringla I. *Islenzk Fornrit XXVI* (1941). Reykjavík.

Almgren, Bertil 1957. Till frågan om de T-formade redskapens användning och därmed sammanhängande näringsförhållanden (On the question of the T-formed implements and associated economic conditions. *Tor:*7-26. Uppsala.

Arwidsson, G. and Berg, G. 1983. *The Mästermyr find. A Viking Age tool chest from Gotland.* Stockholm.

Baudou, Evert 1977. Den förhistoriska fångstkulturen i Västernorrland. In
Baudou, E. and Selinge, K: *Västernorrlands förhistoria* (Prehistory of Västernorrland admin. county), 11-152. Härnösand.

Baudou, Evert 1992. *Norrlands forntid -ett historiskt perspektiv* (The prehistory of Norrland- a historical perspective). Höganäs.

Carpenter, Steven 1991. Fra undervannsarkeologi til maritim arkeologi. Forskningshistorisk tilbakeblikk og nye muligheter (From underwater archaeology to maritime archaeology. A retrospective survey and new possibilities). Unpublished (hovedfagsavhandling i arkeologi). Tromsø.

Decaens, J. 1971. Un nouveau cimitière du Haut Moyen Age en Normandie, Hérouvillette (Calvados). *Archéologie Médiévale* 1, 1-126. Caens.

Farre, Rowena 1954. *Seal morning.*

Granlund, Åke 1962. Nylandsleden av danska itinerariet. *Namn og Bygd.* Uppsala

Hallström, Gustaf 1910. Båtar och båtbyggnad i ryska lappmarken (Boats and boatbuilding in Russian Lapland). *Fataburen 1909,* 85-100. Stockholm.

Hallström, Gustaf 1941. Björnhuvudskulpturen från Arnäs i Ångermanland (The bear head sculpture from Arnäs in Ångermanland). *Ångermanland 1940-41,* 7-40. Härnäsand.

Hødnebø, F. and Magerøy, H. (eds) 1979. *Norges konungasagaer* (The Royal Sagas of Norway) 1. Oslo.

Karman, Jorma 1989. Skifferkultur i centrala Skandinavien. *Populär Arkeologi n° 2,* 16-23. Lund.

Kobylinski, Zbigniew 1988. Things as symbols: the boat in the early medieval culture of northern Europe. In: *Archeologia Polona XXVII,* 185-200. Wroclaw.

Ohlmarks, Åke 1947. *Svenskarnas tro genom årtusendena* (Beliefs of the Swedes through past millennia), Stockholm.

Santesson, O. B. 1941. Magiska skifferred från Norrlands stenålder (Magic slate implements from the Stone Age of Norrland). *Arctos Sverica 1. Studia selecta res vetustas illustrantia ed Oskar Lundberg.* Stockholm/Uppsala. Summary in German.

Solberg, O. 1910. *Eisenzeitfunde aus Ostfinnmarken.* Christiania.

Stenvik, Lars 1980. Samer og nordmenn sett i lys av et uvanlig gravfunn fra Saltenområdet. *Viking 43, 1979.* Oslo.

Taavitsainen, Jussi-Pekka 1978. Hällristningarna-en ny vinkel på Finlands förhistoria (Rock carvings- a new angle towards the prehistory of Finland). *Antropologi i Finland n° 4,* 179-195. Helsinki.

Tilley, Christopher 1991. *Material Culture and Text. The Art of Ambiguity.* London.

Westerdahl, Christer 1985. Förhistoria nolaskogs. Fornlämningar och fornfynd i Örnsköldsviks kommun (The prehistory of northern Ångermanland. Ancient monuments and archaeological finds in the township of Örnsköldsvik). Bjästa.

Westerdahl, Christer 1987. "Et sätt som likna them uti theras öfriga lefnadsart". Om äldre samiskt båtbygge och samisk båthantering ("A way that resembles them in their other customs. On early Saamish boatbuilding and boat handling). *Skrifter utgivna av Johan Nordlander-sällskapet n° 11.* Umeå. Diss.

Westerdahl, Christer 1989. En kulturgräns nolaskogs (A cultural border in northern Ångermanland). *Örnsköldsviks museums småskriftserie n° 20.* Örnsköldsvik.

Wright, Edward V. 1984. Practical experiments in boatstitching. In McGrail, S. (ed): *Aspects of Maritime Archaeology and Ethnography. Papers based on those presented to an international seminar held at the University of Bristol in March, 1982. National Maritime Museum:* 57-84. Greenwich.

# CONTRIBUTORS

| | |
|---|---|
| Béat Arnold | Musée cantonal d'archéologie, Avenue du Peyrou 7, CH-2000 Neuchâtel, Switzerland |
| Martin Bell | Department of Archaeology, Saint David's University College, Lampeter SA48 7ED, Wales |
| John Coates | Sanbinal, Lucklands Road, Bath BA1 4AU, England |
| Bryony Coles | Department of History and Archaeology, The University, Exeter EX4 4QH, England |
| John Coles | WARP, c/o Department of History and Archaeology, The University, Exeter EX4 4QH, England |
| Dale Croes | Department of Anthropology, Washington State University, Pullman WA 99164-4910, U.S.A. |
| Øle Crumlin-Pedersen and Flemming Rieck | The Danish National Museum, Institute of Maritime Archaeology, Strandengen 37, Postbox 304, DK-4000, Roskilde, Denmark |
| Paul Davies and Robert van de Noort | Humber Wetlands Project, School of Geography and Earth Resources, The University, Hull HU6 7RX, England |
| Valerie Fenwick | The Riverbank House, River Road, Taplow SL6 0BG, England |
| Henry Forssell | Stenhagsstigen 1A, SF-00310 Helsingfors, Finland |
| Edwin Gifford | Carlton House, Woodlands, Southampton SO4 2HT, England |
| David Goddard | The Mill, Lympstone, Exmouth EX8 5HD, England |
| Damian Goodburn | 8 Duvards Place, Borden, Sittingbourne ME9 8LJ, England |
| Veryan Heal | Exmoor National Park, Exmoor House, Dulverton TA22 9HL, England |
| Gillian Hutchinson | National Maritime Museum, Greenwich, London SE10 9NF, England |
| Eric Kentley | National Maritime Museum, Greenwich, London SE10 9NF, England |
| Nigel Nayling | Glamorgan-Gwent Archaeological Trust, Ferryside Warehouse, Bath Lane, Swansea SA1 1RD, Wales |
| Keith Parfitt | 8 Castle Avenue, Dover CT16 1HA, England |
| Francis Pryor and Maisie Taylor | Fenland Archaeological Trust, Sycamore Farm, Seadyke Bank, Wisbech St Mary PE13 4SD, England |
| J-P Taavitsainen | National Board of Antiquities, Department of Archaeology, Box 913, SF-00101 Helsinki, Finland |
| Janne Vilkuna | University of Jyväskylä, Seminaarikatu 15, SF-40100 Jyväskylä, Finland |
| Christer Westerdahl | Institute of Prehistoric and Classical Archaeology, University of Copenhagen, Vandkunsten 5, DK-1467 Copenhagen K, Denmark |